Impact Issues 2

Richard R. Day

Joseph Shaules

Junko Yamanaka

Series Editor

Michael Rost

PEARSON

Longman

Published by
Pearson Longman Asia ELT

20/F Cornwall House
Taikoo Place
979 King's Road
Quarry Bay
Hong Kong

fax: +852 2856 9578
email: pearsonlongman.hk@pearson.com
www.pearsonlongman.com

and Associated Companies throughout the world.

This book was developed for Pearson Longman Asia ELT by Lateral Communications Limited.

First published 2009
Reprinted 2011

Produced by Pearson Education Asia Limited, Hong Kong
SWTC/08

Project Director: Michael Rost
Project Editor: Allison Gray
Art Director: Keiko Kimura
Text Designer: Cindy Potter
Video Producer: Todd Rucynski
Production Coordinator: Richard Whitbread
Audio Engineer: Glenn Davidson
Website Coordinator: Keiko Kimura
Photographs: Bananastock, Blue Moon, Brand X Pictures, Dynamic Graphics, Getty Images, Iconotect, Inmagine.

Acknowledgements

The authors and editors of the series would like to thank the following people who provided reviews and piloting reports that aided us in developing *Impact Issues*:

Benjamin Anderson	Suzy Connor	Louise Haynes	Kelly McClusky	Daniel Shin
Steve Andrews	Carol Ann Edington	Tien-Hsin Hsin	Niall O'Reilly	Richard Snelson
Jared Betts	Rebecca Elliott	Stella Hsu	Wayne Allen Pfeister	Laurie Stuart
Michelle Bird	Brett Elphick	Sylvia Hsu	Lesley Riley	Daniel Thach
Joshua Borden	Minyih Christine Feng	Hideko Ino	Jason Rinaldi	Joe Walther
Claude Carone	Glen Gainer	Aaron Jolly	Eric Ritholz	Margaret Yamanaka
Robert Casanova	Timothy J. Gawne	John Jurcin	Cameron Romney	Candace Yu
Marilyn Cawley	Doreen Gaylord	Tomoko Kato	Christopher Ruddenklau	
Li-ching Chen	Greg Goodmacher	Linda Kilpatrick-Lee	Stephen Ryan	
Charles Chon	Ken Hartmann	Arram Kim	Scott Scattergood	
Jude Chung	Mark Hawking	Tae Lee	Helen Seo	

We would also like to thank our colleagues at Pearson Education for their ongoing support, feedback, and guidance. We especially wish to thank Rachel Wilson, Richard Whitbread, Tom Sweeney, Eric Vogt, Katherine MacKay, SunMi Ma, Jan Totty, Serene Chiu, Borys Diakonow, Adrienne Glad, Michael Tom, and Steve King.

IMPACT ISSUES 1
Student Book with Self-Study CD ISBN 978-962-01-9930-1

IMPACT ISSUES 2
Student Book with Self-Study CD ISBN 978-962-01-9931-8

IMPACT ISSUES 3
Student Book with Self-Study CD ISBN 978-962-01-9932-5

Introduction

Impact Issues 2 is part of a 3-book series (*Impact Issues 1, Impact Issues 2, Impact Issues 3*) designed to help students develop conversation and discussion skills. *Impact Issues 2* is a complete course in oral communication for students at a high-beginner to low-intermediate level of English proficiency. It is a collection of 20 exciting and timely topics that students enjoy discussing. Each of the 20 units is carefully presented with activities designed to help students understand the topics, express their own points of view and opinions, and make short presentations.

Learning Philosophy

The *Impact Issues* series has developed a unique *content-based* and *student-centered* approach to language learning. The situation or story in each unit represents a *theme* that students reflect upon, discuss, and share their points of view about. The themes represent **personal issues**, such as life goals, ethics, friendships, romantic relationships, family ties, and jobs, as well as **social issues** such as equal rights, globalization, nationalism, environmental concerns, conflict and peace, refugees, and education.

The activities in *Impact Issues* are intended to help students develop in four key areas of language learning: comprehension, critical thinking, self-expression, and motivation.

Comprehension

Comprehension is the basis for all language development. The *Impact Issues* series helps students increase their comprehension ability through both **reading** and **listening**. Each unit is set up so that students can engage their **background knowledge**, work at identifying main ideas and supporting evidence, and **make inferences** about the speakers' points of view. Throughout the course, students are exposed to a wide range of speaking and self-expression styles and varieties of **international English**.

Critical Thinking

Critical thinking is the ability to **think deeply**, to go beyond explicit information. The *Impact Issues* series helps students develop and use the skills of **comparing information** from complementary sources and reflecting on **personal experience**. Each unit series focuses on both critical thinking skills and critical thinking attitudes.

Critical thinking skills enable students to weigh **different sides of an issue** and arrive at a fair judgment. Critical thinking attitudes allow students to show respect for others' opinions, appreciating **diverse values** and viewpoints and gain the **confidence** to think through an issue.

Self-Expression

Self-expression is the core of a communicative approach to language learning. The *Impact Issues* series focuses on both **discussion** and **presentation** skills.

The heart of each unit is the **sharing** of opinions with classmates, which includes conversation strategies such as soliciting ideas, getting **clarification** and **confirmation**, expressing levels of agreement, and adding evidence and examples to support students' own ideas.

Each unit concludes with a **short personal presentation**, to allow students to feel the power of self-expression in a new language. Students are guided in planning what to say, taking notes, outlining their ideas, and rehearsing.

Motivation

As students go through the process of understanding the issues, reflecting on the issues, discussing different points of view, and sharing their ideas, they will gain **communicative confidence**. Since the students are giving their personal point of view about the topics discussed, they gain a sense of **language ownership**—the sense that they can use English for meaningful communication. This makes the experience of studying English with *Impact Issues* motivating, so that students will want to **extend their communication** beyond the classroom.

Using *Impact Issues*

The units in *Impact Issues* are designed to be accessible linguistically, while challenging the students intellectually. *Impact Issues* is especially suitable for learners whose reading, grammar, and vocabulary skills are greater than their oral production skills. Each unit features a step-by-step preparation that turns students' passive knowledge into active communication practice.

Each unit has these sections:

Getting Ready

Estimated time: **5 minutes**

- Introduces the topic and gets students thinking about their ideas and opinions about the topic.

- Students can work in pairs, taking turns asking and answering the questions. Alternatively, teachers can discuss the questions with the whole class.

Situation

Estimated time: **10-20 minutes**

- Presents the main issue of the unit.

- Students can read the story and listen to it on the Self-Study CD at the same time.

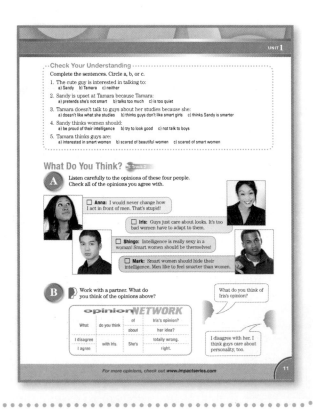

Check Your Understanding

Estimated time: **5 minutes**

- Checks students' understanding of key points.

- Students work in pairs to answer focus questions about the Situation.

What Do You Think?

Estimated time: **10 minutes**

- Helps students understand different perspectives and formulate their own opinions.

- Students work in pairs to share their opinions and expand ways of giving and responding to opinions (Opinion Network).

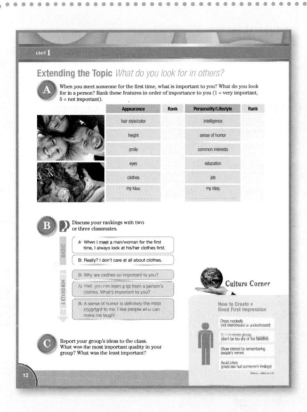

Extending the Topic

Extending the Topic *What do you look for in others?*

Estimated time: **10-15 minutes**

- Lets students connect the unit topic to broader issues and develop critical thinking.

- Students interact in a variety of communication formats: surveys, opinion exchanges, role plays, and debates.

Culture Corner

Estimated time: **5-10 minutes**

- Links the unit theme to a current topic.

- Students discuss cultural topics.

Sharing My Ideas

Estimated time: 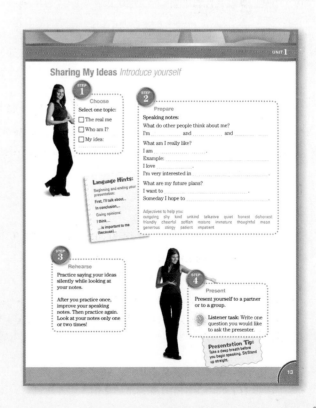 **20-30 minutes**

- Provides support for students in sharing ideas, in pairs or groups.

- Students work through 4 clear steps to prepare short presentations:

  1. **Choose:** select a topic of personal interest.

  2. **Prepare:** answer focus questions, complete charts and graphs, and write notes to make their ideas more specific.

  3. **Rehearse:** work in pairs to practice short presentations and give feedback to their partners.

  4. **Present:** present ideas again, to a new partner or to a larger group, while listeners complete a task.

In the Appendix

Personal Opinions

- Provides unrehearsed opinions from a variety of speakers about each unit topic.
- Students complete a cloze exercise for the opinion summary. Full video clip available at www.impactseries.com/issues.

Vocabulary

- Provides additional vocabulary items and extended definitions of key words and phrases from the unit.
- Students study definitions from *Longman Dictionary of Contemporary English*.

Supplementary Resources

The *Impact Issues* support website (www.impactseries.com/issues) contains

- Unit-by-unit teaching tips

- Unit tests, semester tests, and final tests

- Commentary on units by the individual authors

- Inspirational monographs by the authors on the teaching of skills and development of successful learning attitudes and strategies

- Video clips of fluent English speakers giving extended opinions about each topic in *Impact Issues*

- Links to Internet sites that help teachers develop their own thinking about the topics in *Impact Issues* and that help students explore these topics further.

To the Student

Impact Issues will help you express your opinions and discuss topics in English *successfully*. You will also become confident in presenting your ideas and opinions. The topics and the situations are so interesting that you will want to say something. When you have something you really *want* to say, you learn to speak to the best of your ability.

Here are some tips to help you use *Impact Issues:*

Situation

- Imagine yourself in the situations and stories. How would you feel? What would you do? How can you solve the issue?
- Listen to the Self-Study CD. Think about each speaker's point of view.

What Do You Think?

- Listen to the opinions on the CD. Try to understand their ideas and feelings.
- Give your own opinion. Don't worry about making mistakes.
- Express your true feelings and talk about your own experiences. This is real communication.

Extending the Topic

- Study the example questions and responses. Memorize the patterns.
- Try new vocabulary and new phrases when you talk about your own opinions.
- Listen to new ways that people express their ideas.

Sharing My Ideas

- Speak up, even when you feel a little nervous! This is the fastest way to gain confidence.
- Challenge yourself! You will be able to make a lot of progress with your English when you try to say more.

Enjoy communicating in English.
By the time you finish Impact Issues, *you will be a powerful communicator!*

Contents

Unit	Synopsis	What Do You Think?	Extending the Topic	Sharing My Ideas
1. First Impressions pages 10–13	Two friends disagree about what men find attractive.	Should women change their true behavior to attract men?	What do you look for in others?	Introduce yourself
2. Traffic Jam pages 14–17	Traffic problems and pollution in large cities.	How can we solve our traffic problems?	How "green" are you?	My daily commute
3. Who Needs the Local Language? pages 18–21	Foreigners disagree about the need to learn the local language.	How important is it to learn the local language?	Becoming international	Travel abroad–the perfect trip!
4. Getting Ahead pages 22–25	A brother and sister disagree about raising children, success, and education.	Should everyone in the family be treated the same?	Selfish parents or loving parents?	Family values
5. Forever Single pages 26–29	A woman argues that it's better to stay single.	What does marriage mean to you?	Stay single or get married?	My future plans
6. What Are Friends For? pages 30–33	A university student doesn't know how to help his friend in need.	Do we sometimes do too much for our friends?	What would you do for a friend?	Introducing my friend
7. What's for Dinner? pages 34–37	Classmates disagree about their professor's warnings on diet and how it affects the environment.	Is it better to be a vegetarian or a meat eater?	Favorite foods	What to eat?
8. Cyber Bullying pages 38–41	A student is being cyber bullied by her classmates.	How can we stop bullying?	What should Trish do?	Asking for advice
9. Taking Care of Father pages 42–45	A couple discusses how to take care of an elderly parent.	How can we take care of our parents and grandparents?	Role play: I'd like to come live with you.	The older generation
10. Why Go to School? pages 46–49	Three international students discuss the meaning of university education.	How should students spend their time at university?	Why go to university?	My priorities in school

Unit	Synopsis	What Do You Think?	Extending the Topic	Sharing My Ideas
11. An International Relationship pages 50–53	A Japanese woman is in love with a Finnish man.	How much should we change our lives for love?	More than love?	Big life decisions
12. Too Little, Too Late pages 54–57	A university student writes a letter from the 21st century.	What can we do to save the planet?	It's not too late to change.	My green resolution
13. Ben and Mike pages 58–61	There is a rumor going around about two best friends.	Should we pay attention to rumors?	Best friends: what's OK?	It's not fair!
14. Government Control pages 62–65	A news report about one country's declining birth rate.	Should the government control the population?	Who should have control?	A new law for my country
15. Living Together pages 66–69	A man disagrees with his girlfriend's ideas about living together before marriage.	Should couples live together before marriage?	Parental influences	Moving in with Kenji
16. Size Discrimination pages 70–73	A large woman decides to accept her body.	How much does our weight affect our health and happiness?	Happiness survey	Self-improvement
17. Who Will Help Them? pages 74–77	A blogger writes about his government's position on refugees.	Who is responsible for helping refugees?	World problems	Let's help!
18. Finding the Right One pages 78–81	Friends email each other about some exciting news.	What is the best way to find the right marriage partner?	Looking for love	My ideal
19. Dress for Success pages 82–85	A parent complains about the lifestyle of her daughter's teacher.	What kind of an example should teachers set?	How should teachers act?	Life lessons
20. A Mother's Story pages 86–89	A killer is put to death and the victim's mother is happy.	Do murderers deserve to die?	Just punishment	You be the judge!

Appendix:

1. **Personal Opinions**—extra opinions about the topic of each unit. Corresponds to video clips available on the course website, www.impactseries.com/issues.
2. **Vocabulary**—expanded vocabulary items and definitions for each unit.

9

Situation   Track 1

Sandy and Tamara are at a party and have been talking to a cute guy. After the guy leaves, Sandy is upset at Tamara. Listen to their conversation.

Dave: So, you ladies are students?

Sandy: Yes, I'm a chemistry major.

Dave: That sounds, uh, hard. Are you a student, too?

Tamara: Yeah, just taking a few classes. Enjoying life.

Dave: Oh, cool!

Dave's Friend: Hey, Dave! Come here!

Dave: Uh, I'm sorry, I'll be back. Don't go away.

Sandy: Oh, Tamara, I hate it when you do that!

Tamara: What?

Sandy: Whenever you talk to a cute guy, you hide how smart you are. You said, "I'm just taking a few classes," but you are doing graduate research in physics!

Tamara: Guys don't like it if you sound too smart. Why did you tell them that you're a chemistry major?

Sandy: Because it's true! I want a guy to know that I'm intelligent. But you smile and pretend everything the guy says is brilliant. So they all talk to you and ignore me. It's not fair!

Tamara: It's just flirting.

Sandy: Guys are so predictable. Only interested in a woman's looks. You're smart and beautiful. Don't hide your abilities.

Tamara: Look, guys are afraid of women who are too smart. Besides, it's easier to control the guy if he thinks he's smarter than you are.

Sandy: You're terrible! A real man will appreciate you for your talent, not your looks.

Tamara: Maybe. Oh, look, he's coming back!

Glossary   **Oh, cool!** = Oh, that's great!   **graduate research** = high-level university study   **major** = university student's area of study
brilliant = very smart and interesting   **ignore** = to not pay attention to   **flirting** = showing romantic interest in someone

Check Your Understanding

Complete the sentences. Circle a, b, or c.

1. The cute guy is interested in talking to:
   a) Sandy.   b) Tamara.   c) neither.

2. Sandy is upset at Tamara because Tamara:
   a) pretends she's not smart.   b) talks too much.   c) is too quiet.

3. Tamara doesn't talk to guys about her studies because she:
   a) doesn't like what she studies.   b) thinks guys don't like smart girls.   c) thinks Sandy is smarter.

4. Sandy thinks women should:
   a) be proud of their intelligence.   b) try to look good.   c) not talk to boys.

5. Tamara thinks guys are:
   a) interested in smart women.   b) scared of beautiful women.   c) scared of smart women.

What Do You Think? Track 2

A Listen carefully to the opinions of these four people. Check all of the opinions you agree with.

☐ **Anna:** I would never change how I act in front of men. That's stupid!

☐ **Iris:** Guys just care about looks. It's too bad women have to adapt to them.

☐ **Shingo:** Intelligence is really sexy in a woman! Smart women should be themselves!

☐ **Mark:** Smart women should hide their intelligence. Men like to feel smarter than women.

B Work with a partner. What do you think of the opinions above?

What do you think of Iris's opinion?

I disagree with her. I think guys care about personality, too.

opinion NETWORK

What	do you think	of	Iris's opinion?
		about	her idea?
I disagree	with Iris.	She's	totally wrong.
I agree			right.

Extending the Topic *What do you look for in others?*

**A** When you meet someone for the first time, what is important to you? What do you look for in a person? Rank these features in order of importance to you (1 = very important, 5 = not important).

Appearance	Rank	Personality/Lifestyle	Rank
hair style/color		intelligence	
height		sense of humor	
smile		common interests	
eyes		education	
clothes		job	
my idea:		my idea:	

B Discuss your rankings with two or three classmates.

BASIC

A: When I meet a man/woman for the first time, I always look at his/her clothes first.

B: Really? I don't care at all about clothes.

EXTENSION

B: Why are clothes so important to you?

A: Well, you can learn a lot from a person's clothes. What's important to you?

B: A sense of humor is definitely the most important to me. I like people who can make me laugh!

 **Culture Corner**

How to Create a Good First Impression

Dress modestly.
(not overdressed or underdressed)

Communicate clearly.
(don't be too shy or too talkative)

Show interest by remembering people's names.

Avoid jokes.
(jokes can hurt someone's feelings)

C Report your group's ideas to the class. What was the most important quality in your group? What was the least important?

Source: askmen.com

Sharing My Ideas *Introduce yourself*

STEP 1
Choose
Select one topic:
- ☐ The real me
- ☐ Who am I?
- ☐ My idea:
....

STEP 2
Prepare
Speaking notes:

What do other people think about me?

I'm .... and .... and ....

What am I really like?

I am ....

Example: ....

I love ....

I'm very interested in ....

What are my future plans?

I want to ....

Someday I hope to ....

Adjectives to help you:

outgoing   shy   kind   unkind   talkative   quiet   honest   dishonest
friendly   cheerful   selfish   mature   immature   thoughtful   mean
generous   stingy   patient   impatient

Language Hints:

Beginning and ending your presentation:

First, I'll talk about...

In conclusion,...

Giving opinions:

I think...

...is important to me (because)...

STEP 3
Rehearse
Practice saying your ideas silently while looking at your notes.

After you practice once, improve your speaking notes. Then practice again. Look at your notes only one or two times!

STEP 4
Present
Present yourself to a partner or to a group.

 Listener task: Write one question you would like to ask the presenter.

Presentation Tip:
Take a deep breath before you begin speaking. Sit/Stand up straight.

Getting Ready

Work with a partner.
Answer these questions.

1. How do you get around every day? (bus, train, bicycle, etc.)

2. What are the advantages and disadvantages of each?

Situation Track 3

In many big cities traffic jams create big problems. Listen to the solutions that some cities have found.

In big cities all over the world—Seoul, Taipei, Tokyo, Shanghai, New York, Paris, São Paolo—there is a flood of cars, trucks, buses on the streets. This has caused terrible traffic jams that pollute the air.

But in Singapore there are no traffic jams and its air is free from pollution. In downtown London, traffic circulates more freely than in the past, and in Amsterdam you'll find streets full of bicycles, not cars.

This happy situation is no accident. It is the result of government programs to fight air pollution and traffic jams. Put simply, governments are making it expensive and inconvenient to own a car.

For example, in Singapore, because of taxes and cost of permits, residents might pay over US$250,000 to own a car. And drivers must pay to enter downtown on weekdays. In London, those who drive into the center of the city must pay a per-day fee of up to US$47. In Amsterdam,

owning a car is inconvenient. There are few parking places and the maximum speed limit is only 50 kilometers per hour. Bicycles and trams are more convenient, so many city residents don't even own cars.

What do you think of these systems? They may work, but some people might feel they are not fair. Cars have become so common in our lives that people, rich and poor, feel they have a right to use them.

There might be other problems. Does the public transportation system work well? In some big cities—Los Angeles, for example—the answer is certainly "no." Because the system is so limited, only about 10% of Los Angelenos commute by public transportation. It's easier and faster to drive a car.

Certainly, something must be done to fight pollution and traffic in the world's large cities. What's the solution where you live?

Glossary   **traffic jam** = traffic moving very slowly because there are too many cars   **pollution** = dirty air, water, etc.
inconvenient = difficult   **resident** = person who lives in a particular place   **public transportation** = city trains and buses

··Check Your Understanding··············

Are the sentences true or false? Circle T or F.

1. Every big city in the world has problems with traffic jams.   T / F
2. Traffic problems in Singapore are controlled by making cars expensive.   T / F
3. There are fewer cars in downtown London than there used to be.   T / F
4. The Los Angeles public transportation system sets a good example
   for other large cities.   T / F
5. Cities everywhere can use the same system for controlling traffic.   T / F

What Do You Think? Track 4

 Listen carefully to the opinions of these four people. Who do you agree with most? Rate the opinions from 1 to 4 (1 = strongly agree, 4 = strongly disagree).

☐ **Ken:** Every city should do what these cities have done. It can't be that difficult.

☐ **Susan:** These things are impossible in my city! People love their cars too much.

☐ **Luis:** We should do these things, but only step by step. People don't like change.

☐ **Yeon-Suk:** There are other ways to solve the problem. Let's get rid of gasoline cars and use electric cars!

B Work with a classmate.
Discuss the opinions above.

opinion NETWORK

I	completely	Susan.
	agree with	
	somewhat	Luis.
Whose	opinion	agree with?
	do you	
	idea	think is right?
I	am not sure.	make a good point.
	I think they all	
	don't know.	have good ideas.

I completely agree with Susan. Who do you agree with?

I think Ken is right. Every city should make these changes.

Extending the Topic *How "green" are you?*

A Do you have a car? How do you go from home to these places?
You may check more than one box.

Destination	Car	Taxi	Bus	Train	Subway	Bicycle	Walking
school							
work							
shopping mall							
movies							
friend's house							
favorite restaurant							
grocery store							
other place:							
other place:							

B Compare answers with two or three classmates. Give reasons for your answers. Who is the "greenest" person in your group? Who drives their car the most?

BASIC

A: How do you get to school?

B: I always take the subway. It's the fastest way to get there.
What about you?

EXTENSION

A: I usually walk. I live close by.

C: You're lucky. I have to take the bus. It takes (me) 45 minutes to get here!

C Report your group's results to the class.
Who has the easiest commute?

Culture Corner

The Most *Aggressive* Cities
for Drivers in the U.S.

- Boston
- New York
- Washington, D.C.
- Los Angeles
- Miami

Source: Automobile Association of America

Sharing My Ideas *My daily commute*

STEP 1

Choose

Select a place you commute to every day:

☐ school   ☐ work

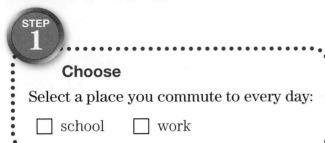

STEP 2

Prepare

Prepare a visual aid. Make a map or diagram that shows your daily commute. Be sure to show your starting point, your ending point, how you get there, and how long it takes.

Speaking notes:

My house

work

walk = 20 minutes

Questions to help you: Do you like your commute?   Why/Why not?   I (like/don't like) my commute because ....
Would you prefer to get to school or work in a different way?

STEP 3

Rehearse

Practice your presentation with a partner. Show your partner your visual aid.

 Listener task: Was the visual aid helpful? Is it missing anything? Tell your partner.

STEP 4

Present

Give your presentation to a new classmate or to a group. Use your visual aid.

 Listener task: How does the presenter's commute compare to your own commute? Faster? Easier? Cheaper?

Presentation Tip:
Make sure your visual is clear and easy to read.

Getting Ready

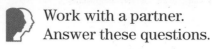

Work with a partner.
Answer these questions.

1. English is an official language in how many countries?
   a) 13   b) 33   c) 53
2. Which two languages have more native speakers than English?
3. What language is spoken by the most people in the world (native and non-native)?

Answers at bottom of page.

Situation Track 5

Peter is an Australian employee who started working in Thailand at a foreign bank. He and his new American colleague Richard discover that they disagree about language learning. Listen to their conversation.

Richard: Peter, I'm going to lunch. Care to join me?

Peter: I'd love to, but I've got my Thai language lesson during lunch hour today.

Richard: Well, I admire your effort. I've been here for four years and I just know the basics.

Peter: Doesn't that create any problems?

Richard: Well, you don't really need to speak Thai to work here. After all, English is the company's working language.

Peter: Well, I used to work in Hong Kong. The local staff spoke excellent English, but I think studying Chinese helped me a lot.

Richard: In theory, I suppose that's true. But foreigners look pretty silly trying to speak such difficult languages. In Thai the pronunciation and the polite language are really hard. I've given up.

Peter: Well, I think the local staff do appreciate the effort. I've seen a lot of problems because foreign staff don't understand local conditions.

Richard: Well, if I need help, I'll just ask one of the local staff. Besides, studying takes so much time. I'd rather spend that time being productive.

Peter: Yeah, it's true. It does take a lot of time.

Richard: Besides, we're in the banking business. Money is something everyone understands. It would increase efficiency more if the local staff spoke better English.

Peter: I don't know. They spend a lot of energy learning English—I think we should do the same.

Richard: Well, that's not going to help them get along in a global world. Anyway, I'm hungry! I'll leave you to your books and go get something to eat.

Peter: OK, enjoy.

"Getting Ready" answers: 1. c   2. Mandarin Chinese and Spanish   3. English

---

Glossary   **Care to** = Would you like to   **admire** = to think something is good or attractive   **In theory** = as some people believe
silly = ridiculous   **appreciate** = to be thankful for   **efficiency** = ability to do something well without wasting time or effort

••**Check Your Understanding**••••••••••••••••••••••••••••••

Answer the questions about Peter and Richard's conversation.

1. Why didn't Peter go to lunch with Richard?

2. How well does Richard speak Thai?

3. What's Richard's opinion of learning the local language?

4. What is the one thing that Richard and Peter agree on?

5. What does Richard think the local staff should do?

What Do You Think? Track 6

 Listen carefully to the opinions of these four people. Who makes the strongest point (even if you disagree)?

☐ **Anna:** It's crazy to live somewhere for four years and not learn the language.

☐ **Shingo:** Why bother to learn the local language when the local staff speaks English?

☐ **Mark:** The local staff should speak better English. It's the language of business.

☐ **Iris:** Native English speakers are spoiled. It's important for them to learn a foreign language.

 Share your opinions with a partner.

opinion**NETWORK**

Anna	has	a clear viewpoint.
		an interesting point.
Shingo		a good argument.
		a strong argument.
Yes,	I think so, too.	
	I believe in the same thing.	
Really?	I don't think so.	
	I don't see it that way.	

Anna has a clear viewpoint. It's important to learn the local language.

Really? I don't think so. English is the international language.

Extending the Topic *Becoming international*

A Here are some ideas about becoming international. Which ones do you think are the most important? Rank these ideas in order of importance (1 = very important, 5 = not important).

Rank	Ways to Become International	What other things can you do to become international? (e.g. travel, study abroad)
	Learn a foreign language that is not English.	....
	Study about the customs of many countries.	....
	Make foreign friends and spend time with them.	....
	Learn about politics and economics.	....
	Learn English. It's the global language!	....

B Compare rankings with a partner. Do you agree?

Extra Activity *Debate*

Work in a group of four. Two of you (A and B) think learning English is the best way to become international. Two of you (C and D) think learning English is not important. Prepare your arguments in pairs (A and B, C and D). Give reasons and examples.

A and B: Give your opinion.
C and D: Explain why you disagree.

> A: We think that learning English is the best way to become international.

> B: It's important because it's the global language. Everybody speaks English.

> C: We disagree. To become international, you must know many things. Not just English.

> D: For example, you should know about world politics and economics. You should also learn about many different cultures, not just English-speaking cultures.

Culture Corner

Are Languages Difficult to Learn?

Here are the top reasons people have trouble learning a foreign language.

- The grammar isn't like my native language.
- There aren't very many similar words.
- It's very different from my native language.
- Sounds and tones are very difficult to hear and produce.
- The writing system is difficult to learn.
- There are very many cultural differences (like level of formality).

Source: language-learning-advisor.com

Sharing My Ideas *Travel abroad–the perfect trip!*

STEP 1

Choose

Select one or two themes for your trip.

☐ Nature ☐ Adventure ☐ Exotic places ☐ Learning ☐ My idea ....

STEP 2

Prepare

Plan your perfect trip. Fill out the following information:

Places I will go ....

How long I will be gone ....

How I will get around ....

Things I'd like to see ....

Things I'd like to do ....

My goals for the trip ....

My ideas: ....

Language Hints:

I'd love to go to...

The reason I want to... is...

Let me tell you about...

STEP 3

Rehearse

With a partner, practice talking about your trip. Try to talk as long as possible.

 Listener task: Give feedback: "I like your idea about... Talk more about that."

STEP 4

Present

Present to a new classmate or to a group.

 Listener task: Answer these questions.
1. Where does the presenter want to go?
2. Why did the presenter choose this place?

Presentation Tip:
Show excitement while you talk!

21

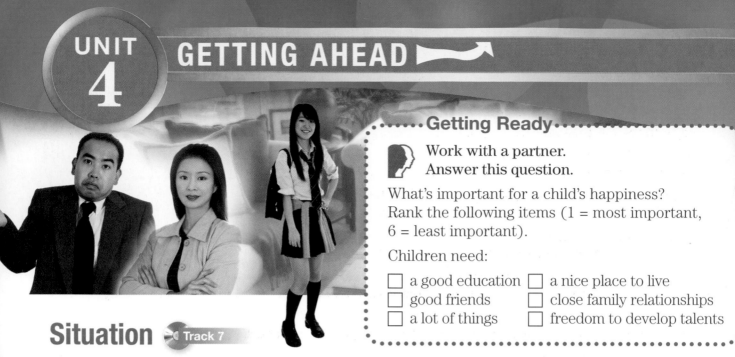

UNIT 4

GETTING AHEAD

Getting Ready

Work with a partner.
Answer this question.

What's important for a child's happiness?
Rank the following items (1 = most important,
6 = least important).

Children need:

☐ a good education   ☐ a nice place to live
☐ good friends   ☐ close family relationships
☐ a lot of things   ☐ freedom to develop talents

Situation   ◖ Track 7

Chao and his sister May are very close, and they usually agree on everything. However, Chao's recent decision to send his daughter Lily to private school has caused a big disagreement. Listen to their conversation.

May: Chao! I need to talk to you about Lily.

Chao: What's the problem? I simply want to send my daughter to a private school.

May: Yes, I'm sure you have good intentions. But you know it will create conflict in the family if Lily gets this special treatment.

Chao: What do you mean? What special treatment?

May: Chao, we don't have the money to send our son to a private school.

Chao: And why not?

May: You know why. All of our money went to buy our new house.

Chao: Fine. You decided to spend your money on a comfortable house. No problem with that. But we want to invest our money in our daughter's education.

May: No, no, no, Chao. It's not so simple. The house is good for the whole family. Wasn't it nice to get together at our house at New Year's?

Chao: Well, yes, it was great. We always enjoy spending time with family. But we just want Lily to get ahead in life, you know.

May: It will create tension. Think how Wei will feel.

Chao: I'm sorry, but we can't hold Lily back because of how you choose to spend your money.

May: Are you suggesting that we were selfish in buying that house?

Chao: No, of course not. But we have to think about our children's future. These days, getting the best education is the only way to be successful.

May: But Lily won't be around our family then. She'll make new friends. She won't want to be around her cousins.

Chao: No, come on. Lily is not going to forget the family. She's a good girl. And she and Wei will still be close. Anyway, we don't plan to stay in this neighborhood forever, either.

May: Oh, are you thinking of moving away from us? That's sad, Chao. Our family comes from here and so many relatives live nearby. We've always been together like one family. We've always done everything together, and your children and our children are so close!

Chao: Well, we have to look towards the future. You're stuck in the past, May.

May: Aggh! You're being selfish. You're not thinking about what's best for the whole family.

Chao: Funny, that's exactly what I was going to say.

Glossary   **get special treatment** = to be treated better than others   **invest in** = to spend your money/time to get something in the future
get ahead = to have success   **be stuck in the past** = to only think about the past

··**Check Your Understanding** ·····································

Complete the sentences. Circle a, b, or c.

1. May and Chao are arguing about:
   a) who has more money.   b) their children's education.   c) spending time together.

2. May isn't going to send her son to a private school because:
   a) it's too expensive.   b) it's too far away.   c) it's not right for the family.

3. Chao is most concerned with:
   a) having a big house.   b) his daughter's education.   c) living close to family.

4. May is worried that Wei and Lily will:
   a) become more competitive.   b) grow apart.   c) not want to see each other anymore.

5. Chao thinks May should:
   a) sell her house.   b) think more about her son's future.   c) move to a better neighborhood.

What Do You Think? Track 8

 A Listen carefully to the opinions of these four people. Who do you agree with most?
Rate the opinions from 1 to 4 (1 = strongly agree, 4 = strongly disagree).

☐ **Yeon-Suk:** Parents need to give their children a good education, even if it causes jealousy.

☐ **Luis:** It's not fair for some family members to be treated differently than others.

☐ **Ken:** Getting into good schools and companies is not what makes families happy.

☐ **Iris:** When children succeed, it helps the whole family.

 B Discuss your ideas with a classmate.

opinion**NETWORK**

I	completely agree		Yeon-Suk.
	agree most		her.
	basically agree	with	Luis.
	kind of agree		him.
	strongly disagree		Ken.
	don't agree at all		him.

I agree most with Luis. Everyone should be treated fairly. What do you think?

I completely disagree with him. I think Yeon-Suk is right.

Extending the Topic *Selfish parents or loving parents?*

A Different families show their love in different ways. Which ways do you agree with (+)? Which ways don't you agree with (–)? Add your own ideas.

To show their love, parents should:

☐ push their children to succeed.   ☐ let children find their own interests.

☐ make children be independent.   ☐ keep children close.

☐ not give children too many things.   ☐ give children many comforts.

☐ show children reality.   ☐ protect their children from the world.

☐ make children work hard.   ☐ let children have fun.

☐ give children a lot of money.   ☐ let children do whatever they want to do.

☐ my idea: ☐ my idea:

....

B Work with two or three classmates. Discuss your ideas. Give examples from your family.

BASIC

> A: Do you think parents should push their children to succeed?

> B: Yes, I do. But they shouldn't push them too hard. Do you agree?

EXTENSION

> A: Not really. I think parents should let children make their own decisions.

> B: Well, I think it's OK sometimes. In my family, my parents tend to push us with our school work, but not with other things.

Culture Corner

C Report your group's ideas to the class. How should parents show their love? Do your classmates agree with you?

Main Concerns with Raising Your Teenage Child

- Drugs/Alcohol
- Education/Future plans
- Morals/Religion
- Social/Peer pressure
- Special Needs
- Jobs/Future goals
- Crime/Violence
- Family/Responsibility
- Sex
- Health/Nutrition

Source: bily.org

Sharing My Ideas *Family values*

 STEP 1

Choose

Select a title for your presentation:

☐ My Family's Values

☐ The Perfect Family

☐ Family Problems!

Language Hints:

• Today, I'm going to talk about . . .

• One example is . . .

• In conclusion, I think . . .

 STEP 2

Prepare

Make an outline. Use these ideas to help you.

Speaking notes:

What do other people think about me?

Introduction (Say what you are going to talk about.)

. . . .

Body (Write your main points and give examples from your family or families you know.)

1st point: . . . .

Example: . . . .

2nd point: . . . .

Example: . . . . , ...

3rd point: . . . .

Example: . . . .

Conclusion: (Say your main idea again, in different words. Give your final opinion.)

. . . .

. . . .

STEP 3

Rehearse

Work with a partner. Practice your presentation once looking at your outline. Practice again without looking.

 Listener task: Did your partner remember everything the second time? Can you give hints to your partner?

STEP 4

Present

Present your ideas to a new partner or to a group.

 Listener task: Fill in the boxes below.

I agree with the speaker's idea that:
I disagree with the speaker's idea that:

Presentation Tip:
Pause between sentences. This will help you keep a good pace.

Getting Ready

Work with a partner.
Answer these questions.

1. In your country, how many people stay single (never get married)?

2. If you decide to stay single, will your parents or relatives pressure you to get married?

Situation Track 9

Angela and her boyfriend have a great relationship. There's just one thing that is keeping them from getting married. Listen to their problem.

Angela doesn't believe in marriage. She has lived with her boyfriend, Luke, for the past two years. Recently, he asked her to marry him, but she said no. She's very happy with Luke the way things are now. She doesn't want to ruin their relationship by getting married, but she loves Luke and she wants to continue living with him.

"Marriage is for fools and dreamers," says Angela. "I mean, who wants to give up her freedom to be with the same man for the rest of her life? Don't get me wrong. I'm not saying people should live alone. I love people, especially men, and that's one reason why I think marriage is not for me. What if I meet someone else who I love more than Luke?"

Angela thinks marriage can change people. "Luke is a great guy. I know he's the type of man many women dream of marrying. He's intelligent and funny. He even does most of the cooking and housework, but what if he changes after we get married? I've seen that happen many times."

Her parents say, "What about children?" Angela doesn't think you need to be married to have children. She says, "I want to have children someday, but I don't need a husband to have a child."

Angela says that people aren't meant to spend all of their lives with one partner. "Look at the divorce rate. Almost half of all marriages end in divorce. And many people who do stay married aren't happy. How many happily married people do you know?"

Angela believes that marriage will die out in the future. "Right now, more and more people live together without being married. There's really no need for marriage," she explains. "I'm going to stay single forever."

Glossary   ruin = to damage, to destroy   **a fool** = a stupid person   **a dreamer** = a person with unrealistic plans for the future   **die out** = to end; to stop

··Check Your Understanding·······

Are the sentences true or false? Circle T or F.

1. Angela and her boyfriend plan to get married in two years.   T / F
2. Angela believes she can have children without being married.   T / F
3. Angela does not want to marry her boyfriend because she does not really love him.   T / F
4. Angela doesn't believe in marriage because people change.   T / F
5. Angela thinks that in the future people will no longer get married.   T / F

What Do You Think? Track 10

 A Listen carefully to the opinions of these four people.
Check all of the opinions you agree with.

 ☐ **Iris:** If a man and a woman have children, they need to be married.

 ☐ **Anna:** When you get married, you give up your freedom.

 ☐ **Mark:** Marriage is natural. If a man and a woman love each other, they should get married.

 ☐ **Shingo:** Marriage is unrealistic. People aren't meant to be with the same person forever.

 B Work with a classmate.
Discuss the opinions above.

opinion NETWORK

Anna	says		you give up your freedom when you get married.
Mark	believes	(that)	marriage is unnatural.
Shingo	thinks		marriage is unrealistic.
What	do you		think?
			believe?
			say about that?

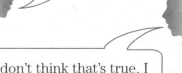

Shingo says marriage is unrealistic. What do you think?

I don't think that's true. I agree with Mark. I think marriage is natural.

Extending the Topic *Stay single or get married?*

 A What do you think of marriage? Which is better, staying single or getting married? Choose your answer (A or B) and the main reason (Check one).

☐ **A. Staying single is good because…**	☐ **B. Getting married is good because…**
☐ many marriages end in divorce anyway.	☐ if you meet the right person, you will live happily together.
☐ when you get married, you have to give up your freedom.	☐ marriages keep society together.
☐ people change. You can't love one person forever.	☐ it's important to bring up children with a mother and a father.
☐ my idea:	☐ my idea:
....	....

 B Next, take a survey. Ask four or five of your classmates what they think of marriage.

Name of classmate	A. Staying single is better	B. Getting married is better	Reason
Emma	☐	☐	wants to keep her freedom
....	☐	☐	....
....	☐	☐	....
....	☐	☐	....
....	☐	☐	....
....	☐	☐	....

 C Report the results in pairs. Ask your partner these questions:

How many people did you interview?

How many chose A?

How many chose B?

What were the main reasons for choosing A? Choosing B?

 ## Culture Corner

Top Reasons to Stay Single

Reason #1: You have a better body. Married people tend to become inactive.

Reason #2: You're more likely to achieve great things. Married people have less free time.

Reason #3: You do less housework. When you're married, you have to spend a lot of time cleaning.

Reason #4: You can do what you want with your money, including keep it.

Source: singletildie.com

Sharing My Ideas *My future plans*

STEP 1

Choose

Select one of the topics:
- ☐ My life 10 years from now
- ☐ My life 20 years from now
- ☐ My life ..... years from now

STEP 2

Prepare

Think of your life 10–20 years from now. Use the questions to help you.

What year is it? .... How old are you? ....

Where do you live? ....

What do you do? ....

Can you tell us about your wife/husband/boyfriend/girlfriend?

....

Do you have children? How many? ....

What is your house like? ....

Can you tell us what you do every day? ....

....

STEP 3

Rehearse

Work with a classmate. Tell your partner your topic. Practice your presentation. Use your notes.

 Listener task: Is there enough information? Do you want to know more?

STEP 4

Present

Present your plan to a new partner or to a group.

 Listener task: Answer these questions: Where does the presenter live? What does he/she do? Is he/she married? Is he/she happy?

Presentation Tip:
After you practice one time, go back and improve your notes.

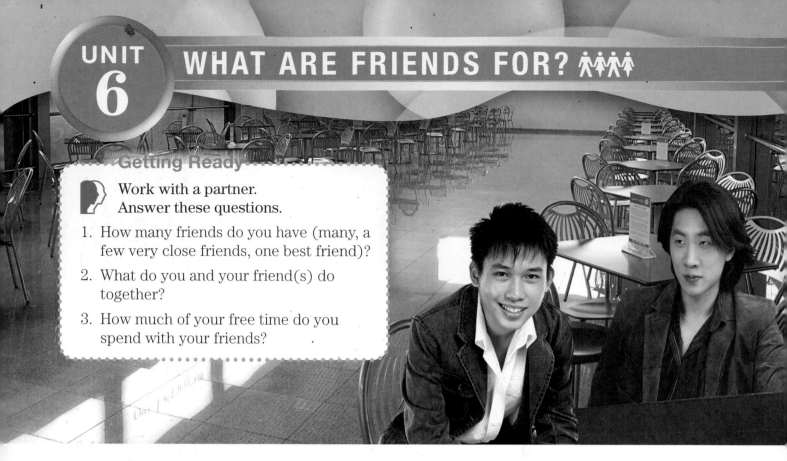

Work with a partner.
Answer these questions.

1. How many friends do you have (many, a few very close friends, one best friend)?

2. What do you and your friend(s) do together?

3. How much of your free time do you spend with your friends?

Situation 🔊 Track 11

Kwan and Sang-Gi are good friends. Sang-Gi is always there for Kwan when he needs help. Now Sang-gi has a serious problem and Kwan doesn't know what to do. Listen to Kwan's problem.

My name is Kwan. I'm a university student. I like to spend time by myself, so I really didn't have any close friends for a long time. But one day I met this guy, Sang-Gi, in the cafeteria and somehow we just hit it off. We got along well, and now we're good friends.

He's really a good guy and I enjoy hanging out with him. We do all kinds of stuff together. We go drinking together on weekends. We go to concerts sometimes. We lend books and DVDs to each other. And we talk about girls!

When I have problems, Sang-Gi's really worried about me. And he always gives me good advice. He just naturally helps me when I'm in trouble. One day my cat escaped from my apartment. I couldn't find her anywhere. Even though I'm sure he was really busy, he came over and helped me look for her. We spent about two hours walking around the neighborhood. Sang-Gi really helps me a lot. When I thank him, he always smiles and says, "Hey, what are friends for?"

These past few days Sang-Gi has looked really depressed. I've asked him what was wrong, but he won't tell me. I keep asking him because I really want to help. Yesterday he finally said that he needed a lot of money, but he wouldn't tell me why. It really seems that if he cannot get the money, probably something horrible will happen to him. I don't know what, but something really bad.

Sang-Gi won't say that he needs help from me. But I want to help him. I have some money I have saved from last summer's part-time jobs. Probably I should lend it to him. Shouldn't I do that? Or should he tell me why he needs the money first? Am I doing too much? I mean, Sang-Gi is my good friend. I want to help him. And I want to smile and say to him, "Hey, what are friends for?"

Glossary **hit it off** = to like someone immediately   **get along well** = to have a good relationship
hang out with someone = to spend time with someone   **lend** = to let someone have/use something for a short time   **depressed** = sad, unhappy

Check Your Understanding

Answer the questions about Kwan and Sang-Gi's situation.

1. How many close friends did Kwan have before he met Sang-Gi?
2. What do Kwan and Sang-Gi like to do?
3. Why does Sang-Gi need money?
4. Why does Kwan want to lend Sang-Gi money?
5. Why is Kwan having a hard time deciding what to do?

What Do You Think? Track 12

A Listen carefully to the opinions of these four people. Who do you agree with most? Rate the opinions from 1 to 4 (1 = strongly agree, 4 = strongly disagree).

☐ **Luis:** Kwan should help Sang-Gi because Sang-Gi always helps him.

☐ **Susan:** Sang-Gi should tell Kwan why he needs the money.

☐ **Yeon-Suk:** It's wrong to lend a lot of money to your friends. Kwan should ask his family for help.

☐ **Ken:** If Sang-Gi is in trouble, Kwan should help him. It doesn't matter why Sang-Gi needs the money.

B Work with a partner. What do you think of the opinions above?

opinion NETWORK

Do you agree with	Luis?
	Susan?
Yes, I do.	He's absolutely right.
	She's absolutely right.
No, I don't.	He's completely wrong about that.
	She's totally wrong about that.

Do you agree with Luis?

Yes, I do. Sang-Gi helps Kwan, so Kwan should help Sang-Gi.

Extending the Topic *What would you do for a friend?*

A What do close friends do for or with each other?
Check your answer and then give a reason.

Situation	Yes	Maybe	Never	Why?
lend each other money				
lend their cars to each other				
invite each other to their homes				
lend each other their clothes				
share an apartment				
tell each other secrets				
talk about sex				
share a drink from the same glass				
ask for advice about a serious problem				
travel to another country				
my idea:				
my idea:				

B Share your answers with two or three classmates. Do you have the same ideas about friendship? Give examples from your own friendships.

BASIC

A: Do you think close friends should share an apartment?

B: No, I don't think it's a good idea. Living together can ruin a friendship.

EXTENSION

A: Really? I live with my best friend and we get along really well.

C: I think it's OK sometimes. It depends on the friends.

Culture Corner

Top Ten Friendship Qualities

A good friend must:

1. be trustworthy
2. be loyal
3. be honest
4. have a sense of humor
5. be fun
6. be dependable
7. have similar interests
8. be kind
9. be a good listener
10. be intelligent

C Report your group's ideas to the class. Which ideas about friendship did your group agree/disagree on?

Source: smartgirls.org

Sharing My Ideas *Introducing my friend*

STEP 1

Choose

Select one topic:

☐ My oldest friend
☐ My newest friend

Language Hints:

My friend is...

We met ____ years/ months/weeks/days ago.

We met at...

We both like...

We like to...

My favorite thing about _____ is...

STEP 2

Prepare

Think about your oldest or newest friend.
Make notes to help you talk about your topic.

Speaking notes:

What is your friend's name? ....

When did you meet? ....

Where did you meet? ....

Do you and your friend have a lot in common? What?

....

What do you like to do together? ....

....

What do you like most about your friend? ....

....

STEP 3

Rehearse

Practice your presentation with a classmate.

 Listener task: Would you like to know more about your classmate's friend? Ask questions.

STEP 4

Present

Present your friend to a new partner or to a group.

 Listener task: Answer these questions.
1. How long have they known each other?
2. How did they meet?

Presentation Tip:
Write brief notes to give your presentation.
Don't write out complete sentences.

Situation · Track 13

Two university students are talking about a lecture by Professor Heidi Cornfield on eating meat and its impact on the environment. Listen to their conversation.

Ethan: I thought Professor Cornfield's lecture was really great! I didn't know that we don't need to eat meat to live.

Maya: Really? You liked her lecture? I wanted to leave class early. I love meat. In fact, I'm going to have a hamburger for lunch.

Ethan: Did you pay attention? Were you sleeping? She said that eating meat hurts, even destroys, the environment.

Maya: Maybe, but that's only her opinion. You know, we humans have always eaten meat. It's part of our nature. It's what we do. I don't understand her opinion that eating meat hurts the environment. Humans have always eaten meat.

Ethan: It's more than just Professor Cornfield's opinion. It's a fact that rain forests in Central America are being destroyed in part to export cheap beef to other countries, including our country. And that hamburger you like so much—well, it takes 20 square meters of rain forest for each burger! So not eating that hamburger can help save rain forests.

Maya: Well, that's important! So if I stop eating hamburgers, I'll help save the environment? Is that right?

Ethan: Yes, that's right. Each of us has to think about our environment. Also, eating meat, especially beef, can cause heart disease.

Maya: OK, OK. I've heard that before. And I guess it's true. But we need protein. And protein comes from meat.

Ethan: Professor Cornfield said that we can get protein from other types of food, not just meat. Tofu is rich in protein.

Maya: Tofu! Do you eat tofu?

Ethan: Sometimes. It's pretty good. You should try it!

Maya: No thanks. Tofu's not for me. Maybe I can do something else to help the environment. Now, where can I get a hamburger?

Glossary   **lecture** = class, speech   **environment** = the natural world where people, animals, and plants live   **in part** = partly (not completely)   **export** = to sell to other countries   **protein** = a natural substance that is necessary to the structure and function of all living cells   **be rich in** = to have a lot of

··**Check Your Understanding**··

Complete the sentences. Circle a, b, or c.

1. What does Professor Cornfield say about eating meat?
   a) Humans need it to live.   b) Humans don't need it to live.   c) It is good for human health.

2. How did Maya feel about Professor Cornfield's lecture?
   a) She's not sure because she fell asleep.   b) She wasn't interested in it.   c) She didn't agree with it, but she liked the lecture.

3. According to Ethan, how does not eating beef help the environment?
   a) It stops pollution.   b) It helps save water.   c) It helps save the rain forests.

4. Why does Maya think that eating meat is important?
   a) Meat has protein.   b) Meat tastes really good.   c) Meat doesn't have a lot of calories.

5. In the end, what does Maya decide to have for lunch?
   a) tofu stir-fry   b) a hamburger   c) a salad

What Do You Think? Track 14

 A Listen carefully to the opinions of these four people. Who makes the strongest point? Rate the opinions from 1 to 4 (1 = strongest point, 4 = weakest point).

☐ **Mark:** I'm not going to stop eating meat. It really doesn't matter.

☐ **Shingo:** The real problem is the fast-food industry. They want us to be addicted to meat.

☐ **Iris:** Vegetarians—people who don't eat meat—are healthier than meat eaters.

☐ **Anna:** It's not a big deal to eat a hamburger once in a while, is it?

 B Work with a classmate. Share your opinions.

opinion NETWORK

I think	(that)	Anna's right.
What	about you?	
	do you think?	
	is your opinion?	
I think	so, too.	
I don't think	so.	

I think Anna is right. What about you?

I think so, too. What's wrong with eating a hamburger once in a while?

Extending the Topic *Favorite foods*

A All of the foods below are made from animal products. Which ones are your favorites? Which ones could you give up if you had to? Rank them from 1 to 10 (1 = most favorite, 10 = least favorite). Give your reasons.

Animal Product/Food	Rank	Reasons
hamburger		
steak		
bacon		
cheese		
eggs		
ice cream (milk, eggs)		
pancakes (eggs, milk)		
ham		
chicken		
pizza (cheese)		

B Discuss your favorite foods with two or three classmates.

BASIC

A: I love cheese! I could never give it up!

B: My favorite is bacon. But I could definitely give up ice cream. What about you?

EXTENSION

A: I love ice cream! I could eat it every day.

C: Yeah, it'd be hard to give up ice cream but I could give up hamburgers and steak. I don't really like beef.

Culture Corner

"Super Foods" Everyone Needs

- apricots
- avocados
- raspberries
- cantaloupe
- cranberries
- tomatoes
- raisins
- figs
- lemons

- onions
- artichokes
- ginger
- broccoli
- spinach
- kelp
- bok choy (Chinese cabbage)

C Do you and your classmates share any of the same favorite foods? Report your similarities to the class.

Source: webmd.com

Sharing My Ideas *What to eat?*

STEP 1

Choose

Select one topic:

☐ I can live without hamburgers.

☐ I cannot live without hamburgers.

Language Hints:

I love/like/hate hamburgers because...

My favorite kind of hamburger is...

I usually eat _____ hamburgers a day/week/month/year.

I think/don't think...

STEP 2

Prepare

Answer these questions to help you make notes for your presentation.

Speaking notes:

1. Do you like to eat hamburgers? Why or why not?

2. What's your favorite kind of hamburger? What do you like to put on it?

3. How often do you eat them? How many hamburgers do you eat in a month?

4. Do you think eating hamburgers harms the environment?

5. Can you live without hamburgers? Why or why not?

STEP 3

Rehearse

Work with a classmate. Practice your presentation.

 Listener task: Did you understand your partner's main points? If not, what didn't you understand?

STEP 4

Present

Present your ideas to a new partner or to a group.

 Listener task: Do you agree or disagree with the main points of the presentation?

Presentation Tip:
Use gestures and body language to make your presentation more exciting.

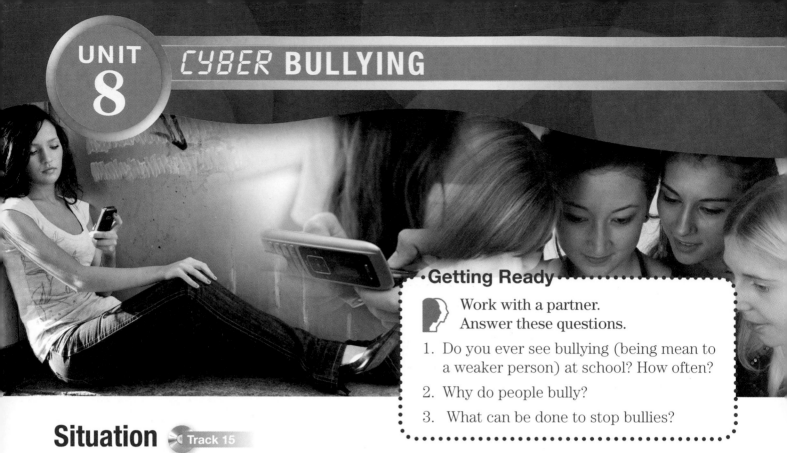

Getting Ready

Work with a partner.
Answer these questions.

1. Do you ever see bullying (being mean to a weaker person) at school? How often?

2. Why do people bully?

3. What can be done to stop bullies?

Situation ◄ Track 15

Trish is a high school student. She has been the victim of some upsetting messages and behavior. Is she being cyber bullied? What should she do? Listen to the conversation between Trish and her friend Shione.

Shione: Trish, you look upset! What's wrong?

Trish: Look at this message on my cell phone.

Shione: "Everybody hates you!" What? Who sent that?

Trish: I don't know. I've had strange things happen lately. Someone posted an embarrassing photo of me onto my blog—taken while I was changing clothes in gym class.

Shione: What? Someone at school did that?

Trish: I don't know who it was. Probably one of the girls at school did it as a joke.

Shione: A joke? That's not funny; that's sick! Anything else?

Trish: Sometimes I've been getting messages like this one—"No one likes you." Or "Your clothes are ugly." But each time the sender is different and I don't recognize them.

Shione: Someone's trying to bully you! Any idea who it could be?

Trish: Not really. One strange thing happened, though. I'm in the tennis circle with Jenna, and she was supposed to send everyone messages about practices. But I never received any—even though everyone else got them.

Shione: Well, did you ask her about it?

Trish: Yeah. She just said that the problem must be with my email account. But I've never had that problem before. And why would Jenna be mean to me? She's one of the most popular people in school.

Shione: Sometimes popular students don't like competition. I really think we need to talk to a teacher or get help figuring out where these messages are coming from.

Trish: No! That will just make things worse. It's probably just a joke.

Shione: Trish, we have to tell someone.

Trish: No, please! Just forget about it.

Glossary **be upset** = to feel bad   **blog** = website—often a personal diary   **that's sick** = that's cruel or mean   **popular** = well liked by many people
competition = act of trying to be better than someone   **figure out** = to find the answer

•••Check Your Understanding•••••••••••••••••••••••

Answer the questions about Trish's situation.

1. Why is Trish upset?

2. What other things have happened to Trish lately?

3. Who is doing things to Trish?

4. What does Shione think Trish should do?

5. What does Trish think she should do?

What Do You Think? Track 16

 A Listen carefully to the opinions of these four people. Who has the best idea? Rank the opinions from 1 to 4 (1 = best idea, 4 = worst idea).

☐ **Susan:** Shione is overreacting. Teenagers play these kinds of jokes all the time.

☐ **Ken:** Sometimes popular people take jokes too far. It's not fair to others.

☐ **Yeon-Suk:** Maybe Trish did something to attract negative attention. She should think about her own actions.

☐ **Luis:** Bullying is wrong and illegal. Trish needs to get help.

 B Discuss the opinions with a classmate.

opinion NETWORK

I	agree with	Susan.	Don't you?
	don't agree with	Ken.	Do you?
No,	absolutely not.		
	I definitely don't.		
Yes,	absolutely!		
	definitely!		

I agree with Susan. Don't you?

No, absolutely not. I think Ken is right. It's really not fair to Trish.

Extending the Topic *What should Trish do?*

 A Think about Trish's problem. Match the advice and the reasons. Add your own ideas.

Advice	Reason
1. Wait a little longer.	☐ Classmates at school may know who is doing it.
2. Ask friends for help.	☐ If she's doing it, she might stop.
3. Tell a teacher or parent.	☐ It's illegal and must be stopped.
4. Contact the cell phone company.	☐ She might learn who sent the messages.
5. Ask Jenna about it.	☐ It's a serious problem and Trish needs help from an adult.
6. Tell the police.	☐ The bullying might stop and it won't be necessary to ask for help.
My idea:	☐ . . . .
My idea:	☐ . . . .

 B Discuss the advice with a partner. Which is the best advice? Worst advice?

Extra Activity *Debate*

Work in a group of four. Two of you (A and B) think Trish should get help. Two of you (C and D) think Trish should wait a little longer. Prepare your arguments in pairs (A and B, C and D). Give reasons and examples.

A and B: Give your opinion.
C and D: Explain why you disagree.

> A: We think Trish should get help immediately. This is a serious problem.

> B: She should talk to a teacher or to a parent before things get worse.

> C: But the bullying might stop.

> D: Yeah, we think it's better to wait a little longer.

Culture Corner

Signs of Being a Bully

1. Do you pick on people who are smaller than you?
2. Do you like to tease or taunt other people?
3. Do you like to see people you tease get upset?
4. Do you think it's funny when people make mistakes?
5. Do you like to take or destroy others' belongings?
6. Do you want other students to think you're the toughest kid in school?
7. Do you get angry a lot and stay angry for a long time?
8. Do you blame other people for things that go wrong in your life?
9. Do you like to get revenge on people who hurt you?
10. When you play a game, do you always have to be the winner?
11. If you lose at something, do you worry about what other people will think of you?
12. Do you get angry or jealous when someone else succeeds?

A bully is someone who answers "yes" to 3 or more of these questions.

Source: The Palo Alto School System, California

Sharing My Ideas *Asking for advice*

Choose

Select one of the topics below:

☐ A time I asked someone for advice

☐ A time someone asked me for advice

Prepare

Make an outline of your story. Use the questions to help you.

Speaking notes:

Title:
Introduction: (Who is the story about? What was the problem? When did this happen?)
Body: (What advice did you get/give?)
Conclusion: (Did the advice help you/that person? How? What happened afterward?)

Language Hints:

Story starters:

This is a story about...

One time, I/_____
had a problem with...

Story endings:

So, in the end...

Finally,...

Rehearse

Tell your story to a partner. Practice two times, once while looking at your outline, and once without looking.

 Listener task: Did your partner forget anything the second time?

Present

Present your story to a new classmate or to a group.

 Listener task: Answer the questions.
1. What's the title of the story?
2. What's the story about?

Presentation Tip:
Remember to put feeling into your voice.
Your story will be more interesting.

Getting Ready

Work with a partner. Answer these questions.

1. Do you have grandparents?
2. How often do you see them?
3. Where do they live? Do they live alone?

Situation 🔵 Track 17

Joo-Kyung's mother died a year ago, and now her 72-year-old father lives alone in an apartment. Joo-Kyung just received a phone call from the owner of the apartment. She's telling her husband some bad news. Listen to their conversation.

Joo-Kyung: Bad news, Kwon. That was Mr. Moon. You know, the guy who owns my father's apartment.

Kwon-Woo: What's up? Is your father OK?

Joo-Kyung: Yes, yes, he's fine. That's not what he called about. Mr. Moon wants my father to move out of his apartment at the end of the month.

Kwon-Woo: What? In 30 days? Why?

Joo-Kyung: I'm not sure. He was very vague about it. Maybe Mr. Moon is afraid my father will die in the apartment.

Kwon-Woo: Oh, and he thinks that would be bad luck… and nobody will want to rent it again?

Joo-Kyung: Yeah, maybe, something like that.

Kwon-Woo: But your father's in good health. Moon can't do that.

Joo-Kyung: Yes, he can. The lease is over at the end of the month.

Kwon-Woo: Oh, yes, that's right. What are we going to do?

Joo-Kyung: Since I'm the only child, we have to take care of him. He will come to live with us.

Kwon-Woo: Here? In this tiny apartment? There are only two bedrooms. We can't move our two sons out of their small bedroom.

Joo-Kyung: What else can we do? I'm his only child. We have to take care of him.

Kwon-Woo: Maybe we could look for a new place to live. A bigger place.

Joo-Kyung: In Seoul? You know that's impossible. We looked last year and everything in this area of the city is too expensive. We need to move away from Seoul. Someplace cheap.

Kwon-Woo: But then I would be far away from my office. It might take me up to two hours on the train. I hate to commute.

Joo-Kyung: OK. The only way is for Father to live with us, here in this apartment.

Kwon-Woo: Impossible!

Glossary **What's up?** = What's happening?/What's going on? **vague** = not clear **lease** = the time period for renting
tiny = very small **commute** = to go back and forth from home to work

··Check Your Understanding ·······················

Answer these questions. Circle a, b, or c.

1. Joo-Kyung's father lives:
   a) by himself.   b) with Mr. Moon.   c) with Joo-Kyung.

2. Mr. Moon probably wants Joo-Kyung's father to move out because he:
   a) wants more money for the apartment.   b) doesn't want anyone to die in the apartment.
   c) doesn't like Joo-Kyung.

3. Joo-Kyung thinks that her father should:
   a) stay in his apartment.   b) live with Kwon and her.   c) find a new apartment.

4. Joo-Kyung thinks they should move away from Seoul, but Kwon:
   a) loves Seoul and refuses to leave.   b) wants to live close to his work.   c) wants to be near his own family.

5. It's important for Joo-Kyung to take care of her father because:
   a) she's the oldest child.   b) she has more money than her brothers.   c) she is an only child.

What Do You Think? Track 18

 Listen carefully to the opinions of these four people. Who do you agree with most?
Rate the opinions from 1 to 4 (1 = strongly agree, 4 = strongly disagree).

☐ **Anna:** I don't see what the problem is. Joo-Kyung and Kwon should find another apartment for her father.

☐ **Mark:** They should move to a larger house away from Seoul. That way everyone can live comfortably.

☐ **Iris:** They should find a nursing home for the father. That's the best solution for everyone.

☐ **Shingo:** Kwon is being selfish. Joo-Kyung's father should move into their apartment with them.

B Discuss your ideas with a partner.

opinion**NETWORK**

What do you think about	Anna's point?
How do you feel about	Mark's opinion?
I'm afraid I can't	agree with her.
I really don't	see his point.
I guess	she makes a good point.
I suppose	he's right.

What do you think of Anna's opinion?

I kind of agree with him. But maybe they can't afford another apartment.

Extending the Topic *Role play: I'd like to come live with you.*

  Work with a partner. You will create a role play. Think about this situation:

Person A = parent (mother or father), about age 65

Person B = child (son or daughter), about age 30

Situation: The parent is now single and retired (doesn't work anymore). He or she wants to come to live with the child.

  Prepare your role play. First, what are advantages and disadvantages of older parents moving in with their children? Think about Joo-Kyung's situation to help you.

Advantages	Disadvantages
more economical (saves money)	*too many people in the house*

  Now create a 1-minute role play between the parent and the child.

Start like this:

A: . . . . , I have an idea. I'd like to come live with you.

B: Really? You want to come live with me? Why?

End like this:

A: So, what do you think? Is it a good idea?

B: . . . .

Culture Corner

Growing Old—What People Fear

- Germany—fear of losing memory and mental capacity
- Thailand—fear of losing eyesight
- Holland—fear of gaining weight
- Belgium—fear of losing control of body functions
- France—fear of losing attractive appearance
- USA—fear of losing independence
- Brazil—fear of losing teeth
- Argentina—fear of losing sexual drive
- Japan—fear of having children worry too much
- India—fear of losing hair

  Perform your role play in front of another pair or in front of the class.

Source: International Longevity Center

Sharing My Ideas *The older generation*

STEP 1
Choose

Who will you talk about? Think of a good story to tell about that person.

☐ My grandmother   ☐ My grandfather   ☐ An older person I admire

STEP 2
Prepare

Make an outline of your story. Use the questions to help you.

Speaking Notes:

Introduction:
(Introduce the person: What's his/her name? Describe him/her. Where does/did he/she live?)
Name: ....
Lived/Lives in: ....
Describe him or her: (what he/she is like)

....
....

Body: (Tell your story: What happened? When did it happen? How old were you?)

....
....
....

Conclusion: (Why is this story special to you? Make a final point about the person.)

....
....

Language Hints:

Introduction

I'm going to tell you a story about...

My grandmother/ grandfather's name is...

Conclusion

This story is special to me because...

As you can see, my grandmother/grand- father is very special because...

STEP 3
Rehearse

Silent practice: Practice saying your ideas silently one time. After practicing once, try to improve your speaking notes and practice silently again.

STEP 4
Present

Present your ideas to a classmate or to a group.

Listener task: Check the things the presenters talk about.

☐ The person's name.
☐ Where the person lived/lives.
☐ How old they were when the story happened.
☐ Why the story/person is special to them.

Presentation Tip:
Always make eye contact with your audience. This shows that you are confident!

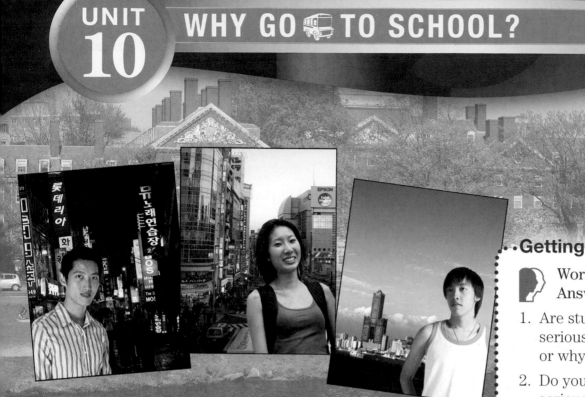

Getting Ready

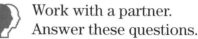

Work with a partner.
Answer these questions.

1. Are students in your country serious? Too serious? Why or why not?

2. Do you think you are a serious student?

Situation 🔴 Track 19

In this month's issue of *Student Voices*, we hear from three university students from Japan, Korea, and Taiwan. We asked these fourth-year university students to give us their opinions about their university experience.

Mariko Ono (Tokyo, Japan): Hi, I'm Mariko. I attend one of the best universities in Japan. When I was in high school, I worked very hard to get into this university. Now that I'm here, I'm enjoying my life. I have a part-time job. I use the money from the job to travel, party, and have fun. I'm taking the minimum number of credits to graduate. Making friends, traveling, enjoying life—these are the things that matter most to me right now. I know that when I graduate, I will get a job and work very hard. So now I want to have a good time!

Lee Jin (Seoul, Korea): Hello, my name is Jin. For me, I want to do very well at my university so I can get a good job after I graduate. To do that, I must get good grades. My life is miserable. I have no social life. No friends. Nothing except my studies. I study all of the time, including weekends and holidays. But I have to work hard. I must do well. I must get a good job when I finish my university studies. This is all I care about. Getting a good job is my goal.

Zhijun Chu (Taipei, Taiwan): I'm Zhijun. I don't have much time to talk. I'm very, very busy. Work, work, work. Study, study, study. This is my life. This has been my life since I entered this university three years ago. But I'm not complaining. I'm not here to make friends and go to parties. I study really hard and have three different part-time jobs for a reason. I'm saving money so that I can start my own company when I graduate. My family is proud of me. I'm doing this for them. I want to succeed in order to honor my parents.

Glossary   **minimum** = least possible amount   **credit** = unit of study (usually equal to 1 hour of class)   **miserable** = very unhappy and sad   **complain** = to express unhappiness about something   **succeed** = to do very well; to reach a goal   **honor** = to show great respect

····**Check Your Understanding**··························

Answer the questions about Mariko, Jin, and Zhijun.

1. Why is Mariko working part-time while studying?

2. What do Jin and Zhijun have in common?

3. Why is Jin miserable?

4. What is each student's plan for after graduation?

Mariko's plan .... Jin's plan .... Zhijun's plan ....

What Do You Think? Track 20

 A

Listen carefully to the opinions of these four people. Who makes the strongest point? Rate the opinions from 1 to 4 (1 = strongest point, 4 = weakest point).

☐ **Ken:** Lee Jin and Zhijun Chu are doing the right thing. They'll both be successful.

☐ **Yeon-Suk:** Mariko is right. We need to enjoy life, especially while we're young.

☐ **Susan:** All three are wrong. We need to have a balance in our lives.

☐ **Luis:** What is Mariko doing? She should be thinking about her future.

 B

Work with a partner.
Talk about the opinions above.

I think Susan has the best argument. What do you think?

Her idea is a bit weak. I think working hard for something is a good thing.

opinion NETWORK

I think	Ken	is right.
	Luis	
Who	do you	agree with?
		think is right?
I	am not sure.	
	really don't know.	

Extending the Topic *Why go to university?*

A

What are the important reasons for going to university?
Put a check next to your top three answers.

Reasons	Reasons
☐ to study, to learn new things	☐ to make their parents happy
☐ to get a good job	☐ to become a good citizen
☐ to get a university degree	☐ to work for a better world
☐ to get qualifications	☐ to be a leader
☐ to find a boyfriend/girlfriend	☐ to enjoy university life

B

Discuss your ideas with two or three classmates.
Reach an agreement on your group's top three choices

BASIC

> A: The main reason why people go to university is to get the degree.

> B: Actually, I think most people go to make their parents happy.

EXTENSION

> C: No way! People go to university to study and learn things.

> D: Well, a lot of people go so that they can get a good job.

C

Report your top three choices to the class.
Do your classmates agree with you?

Extra Activity *Debate*

Work in groups of five. Two of you (Pair A) will be "in favor of" university study: "University study is the most important thing for young people."

Two of you (Pair B) will be "against" university study: "University study is not so important for young people." One of you will be "The Judge."

First, Pair A and Pair B work with your partners. Make a list of your reasons.

Then exchange ideas with the other pair. "The Judge" will decide: who has made the better argument? Why?

Culture Corner

The #1 "Status" Universities in Different Countries

- Harvard University, USA
- University of Cambridge, UK
- Beijing University, China
- National University of Singapore, Singapore
- University of Tokyo, Japan
- University of Hong Kong, Hong Kong
- Seoul National University, Korea
- Universidad Nacional Autónoma, Mexico
- National Taiwan University, Taiwan
- Chulalongkorn University, Thailand

Source: topuniversities.com

Sharing My Ideas *My priorities in school*

STEP 1

Choose

Select three of the priorities from **Extending the Topic**:

☐ Studying ☐ Graduating from university ☐ Part-time jobs ☐ Traveling
☐ Enjoying life ☐ Getting a good job ☐ Meeting people
☐ Finding a boyfriend/girlfriend ☐ My idea: ....

STEP 2

Prepare

Look at the priorities that you chose. Now put them in order from most important to least important. Give your reasons.

Speaking notes:
Introduction: (Say what you are going to talk about.)

Priorities	Reasons
Top priority:	
Second priority:	
Third priority:	

Conclusion: (Make a final statement about your feelings about school.)

STEP 3

Language Hints:

My top priority at school is...
The main reason I go to school is...
This is important to me because...

Rehearse

Practice with a classmate.

 Listener task: Think about your partner's presentation.

- Are there three priorities?
- Is there a reason for each priority?
- How important is school to your partner?

Tell your opinion to your partner.

STEP 4

Present

Present your priorities to a new partner or to a group.

 Listener task: What is the presenter's top priority?

Presentation Tip:
Be sure your notes are brief and well organized before you start your presentation.

Situation 🎧 Track 21

Akane is writing an email from Paris to her best friend Mari back in Japan. She's in love and enjoys what she's doing, but doesn't know what to do about her future! Listen to her email.

Dear Mari,

I feel so much pressure. My course at the Arts College here is almost over. My life has changed so much. Now I'm sure I want to be an artist. But where? Lukus wants me to move to Finland. He's amazing! It feels so natural to be with him. I'm so glad he's in my life! And he's an artistic genius! But live in Finland?

When I visited Helsinki, it was so dark and cold! And Finnish is a really hard language to learn. Lukus says that he can support us while he does art part-time. I could do art full-time! But I would be so alone in Finland, and I don't have connections in the art world like I do back home.

My conversation with Mom was so hard. She and Dad are totally against the idea of me living in Europe. Dad seems to think that since they paid for my studies they can tell me how to live my life. And they are definitely against me marrying a foreigner. That's not fair!

Of course I've only known Lukus for six months. And he doesn't want to live in Japan. What could he do there? We'd have no money. If I have to support him, I wouldn't be able to do my art at all. And my family may not accept him anyway. If I go back alone, I could work part-time, live at home, and do my art, too. But that's not what I want to do. I'm truly in love, and I really want to be with Lukus.

We talked about trying to live in Paris. I'd love that, but how could we make a living? There are thousands of starving artists here. And I can't even get a working visa... unless we got married! But I'm not sure I'm ready for that. I'm so confused.

What should I do? I feel that all of my dreams may be about to come true. Or maybe none of them!

I look forward to hearing from you.

Best,
Akane

Glossary   **genius** = someone who is very smart or talented   **support** = to make money to live   **make a living** = to earn money by working
starving artists = (expression) artists who believe making art is more important than making money

Check Your Understanding

Are the sentences true or false? Circle T or F.

1. Akane is soon going to visit Finland for the first time. T / F
2. Lukus doesn't want to live in Japan. T / F
3. Akane doesn't want to live in Paris. T / F
4. Akane thinks that staying in Paris is the best solution. T / F
5. Akane wants to marry Lukus as soon as possible. T / F

What Do You Think? Track 22

 A Listen carefully to the opinions of these four people. What do you think of Akane's situation? Check the opinions you agree with.

 Shingo: Love is a precious gift. She should go to Finland.

Anna: She should convince Lukus to go to Japan. If he loves her, he will.

Mark: It's clear she's in love. They should get married and try living in Paris.

Iris: To succeed as an artist she'll have to give up Lukus and go back to Japan.

 B Work with a classmate. What do you think of the opinions above?

opinion NETWORK

I	agree most	with	Shingo.
	agree 100 percent		
	kind of agree		Anna.
	sort of agree		
	agree least		Iris.
	completely disagree		

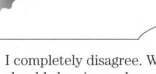

I agree 100% with Shingo. Their relationship is more important than her career.

I completely disagree. Why should she give up her career? They should compromise and stay in Paris.

Extending the Topic *More than love?*

A Is love enough to make any relationship work? Are these things big problems or not? Mark your answers.

Imagine: the person I love...	A big problem	A small problem	No problem!
comes from a different country.	☐	☐	☐
doesn't get along with my family.	☐	☐	☐
doesn't have a job.	☐	☐	☐
doesn't speak my language well.	☐	☐	☐
doesn't agree about having children.	☐	☐	☐
is ten years older than me.	☐	☐	☐
doesn't share the same interests as me.	☐	☐	☐
doesn't have the same ideas about money as me.	☐	☐	☐
my idea:	☐	☐	☐

B Discuss the problems with two or three classmates. Talk about what makes a relationship work.

BASIC

A: What if the person you love comes from a different country?

B: That's definitely a problem because communication is more difficult.

EXTENSION

C: I think it can be a big problem. There are cultural differences too.

A: It depends on the countries. Maybe it's no problem at all.

Culture Corner

Obstacles and Challenges for International Marriages

Some of the problems these relationships face include:

- Language barrier
- Differences in values
- Religious conflicts
- Gender expectations
- Handling finances
- Fear of abandonment by family, friends, spouse
- Political issues

C Report your group's ideas to the class. According to your group, which relationship situation is the biggest problem?

Source: counselors Sheri and Bob Stritof (about.com)

Sharing My Ideas *Big life decisions*

Sometimes you have to make big decisions in life. Imagine that you have met the perfect man/woman or that you have found the perfect job. But you have to make big changes in your life for this person or job. What changes would you be willing to make? What changes would you refuse to make?

STEP 1

Choose

What would you do for:

☐ love? ☐ the perfect job? ☐ my idea: ....

STEP 2

Prepare

Answer these questions to help you make notes for your presentation.

What I would do for ....

I would...	I wouldn't...
....	....
....	....
....	....

Some questions to help you: Would you... leave your family? move to a foreign country? learn a new language? commute a long way?

Language Hints:

For _ ___, I would be willing to...

For _____, I don't mind...

For _____, I would give up...

Even for ____, I would not...

STEP 3

Rehearse

Practice your presentation with a classmate.

Listener task: Is the presentation clear? Do you understand your partner's main points?

STEP 4

Present

Present your ideas to a new partner or to a group.

Listener task: Would you do the same things for love/ a job/other?

Presentation Tip:
Be a good listener. Take notes during your classmates' presentations.

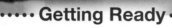

Getting Ready

Work with a partner.
Which of these statements is true?

1. Paper products make up 40% of all trash.

2. Americans throw away 2.5 million plastic bottles every hour.

3. Cell phones, computers, and other gadgets release toxins into the environment when they are thrown away.

Answers at bottom of page.

Situation Track 23

It's 100 years in the future. Joe is studying world history. He doesn't like what he's learning. Listen to his history lesson.

My name is Joe. I'm a university student studying the history of the early 21st century. The more I read, the more I learn, the more angry and upset I get. I keep thinking, "What was wrong with people then? Why didn't they listen? Were they stupid?"

In the history books there are photographs of the Earth in 2020, just before the Earth really warmed up. It was beautiful! Green forests, blue oceans! Really beautiful. But look at the Earth now. Gray. Everything is gray.

People had been warned. Scientists showed how the Arctic ice cap was melting, how the oceans were rising, how the Earth was getting warmer and warmer.

I read in one book about recycling. Some countries, like Japan, had good recycling programs. But other countries, including some of the major polluters, like the United States, didn't do much. I also read that some politicians didn't believe the scientists! How stupid! Why would the scientists lie?

Moreover, I read that some countries were too busy fighting wars to pay attention to climate change. They didn't want to spend the money. And then some countries were developing rapidly—moving from being poor to being wealthy. And that caused a lot of pollution, as the people started driving cars and using air conditioners and polluting rivers.

So look at us now, 100 years later. The Earth is wasted—there is very little clean water and not much food to eat. In my city, we have electricity only six hours a week. We walk or ride our bicycles everywhere because no one is allowed to drive cars, trucks, or buses. And ordinary people can't use airplanes, either. So basically, I'm going to live and die in the same city I was born in.

So I would like to thank everyone who was living 100 years ago for doing so little. For being blind and deaf. For ruining Earth. Now it's too late.

"Getting Ready" answers are all true.

Glossary   **ice cap** = a very large area of thick ice   **deaf** = unable to hear   **blind** = unable to see
climate change = change in the weather on Earth over long periods of time   **wasted** = ruined, destroyed

•••Check Your Understanding•••••••••••••••••••••••••••••••

Answer these questions about Joe's history lesson.

1. According to Joe, what did people do wrong in the 21st century?
2. Why did some countries ignore global warming?
3. Did people know about global warming in the early 21st century?
4. What is wrong with the Earth in Joe's time?
5. Is life easy or hard for people in the 22nd century?

What Do You Think? Track 24

 A Listen carefully to the opinions of these four people. Who makes the strongest point? Rate the opinions from 1 to 4 (1 = strongest point, 4 = weakest point).

☐ **Yeon-Suk:** Everyone should stop using disposable products such as paper cups and wooden chopsticks. They destroy forests and increase garbage.

☐ **Luis:** We should ban people from driving cars for eight hours every day. Cars cause air pollution and increase global warming.

☐ **Ken:** We need to use the energy from the sun. Solar power is cheap and clean.

☐ **Susan:** We need to control the population. There are simply too many people on the Earth. Fewer people means less demand on our limited natural resources.

 B Share your opinions with a partner.

opinion NETWORK

I think	Ken	has the best argument.
	Susan	has the right idea.
What	do you think?	
	is your opinion?	
If you ask me,	his argument is	a bit weak.
	her idea doesn't	make sense to me.

I think Yeon-Suk has the best argument. What do you think?

Her idea is OK. But it's not enough. We need to do more.

Extending the Topic *It's not too late to change.*

 A Changing our lifestyles can help save the environment. Look at these suggestions. Do you think they are possible?

Lifestyle change	Easy to do	Hard to do	Impossible
Use less gasoline. (Drive less. Walk or ride your bike more.)			
Use solar or electric cars.			
Use less electricity. (Don't leave the lights on. Turn off or unplug electric appliances when you're not using them.)			
Eat less meat. (This uses less forest land for cattle.)			
Stop using disposable products. (Take cloth bags to the grocery store.)			
Reuse plastic bags, bottles, and containers.			
Recycle more.			
Use less water. (Turn off water when brushing teeth. Take shorter showers.)			
Control the population.			

B Talk about lifestyle changes with two or three classmates. Which changes do you agree on?

Extra Activity *Debate*

 Work in a group of four. Two of you (A and B) think changing your lifestyle can help the environment. Two of you (C and D) disagree. Prepare your arguments in pairs (A and B, C and D). Give reasons and examples.

A and B: Give your opinion.
C and D: Explain why you disagree.

> A: In our opinion, changing our lifestyles can help save the environment.

> B: We think individuals can make a big difference.

> C: We don't think this is realistic. It just isn't possible for some people.

> D: For example, many people have to drive every day.

 **Culture Corner**

Futuristic Movies
Here are some popular films about the future:

- *Modern Times* (1936)
- *The War of the Worlds* (1953)
- *Farenheit 451* (1966)
- *2001: A Space Odyssey* (1968)
- *A Clockwork Orange* (1971)
- *Mad Max* (1979)
- *Blade Runner* (1982)
- *Back to the Future* (1985)
- *Star Trek* (1986)
- *Aliens* (1986)
- *Akira* (1988)
- *Star Trek* (1989)
- *The Matrix* (1999)
- *Planet of the Apes* (2001)
- *Stargate* (2002)
- *I, Robot* (2004)

Source: rateitall.com

Sharing My Ideas *My green resolution*

Make a resolution (a decision to do something) to help the environment.

STEP 1

Choose

Select your resolution. Choose more than one if you want.

From now on, I'm going to ☐ reduce. ☐ reuse. ☐ recycle.

Language Hints:

I have made up my mind that...

I have decided that I will...

From now on, I will...

I'm going to start...

STEP 2

Prepare

Make some notes about your presentation. Use the questions to help you.

Speaking notes:

Usually, I...	But from now on, I...

Questions to help you:
How often do you use disposable products? How often do you drive your car? How often do you use an air conditioner?
Do you recycle paper, cans, or bottles? Do you use a lot of water? How often do you eat meat?

STEP 3

Rehearse

Practice with a partner.

Listener task: Take notes. What are your partner's resolutions?

STEP 4

Presentation Tip:
Smile at your audience. Remember to relax.

Present

Present your resolutions to a new classmate or to a group.

Listener task: Write down one question you would like to ask the presenter about his/her resolution.

Getting Ready

Work with a partner.
Answer these questions.

1. Why do people "spread rumors" (tell stories about someone that may or may not be true)?

2. Do you believe everything that people tell you? Why or why not?

3. How much do you care about what others say about you?

Situation ◖ Track 25

This is a story about Ben and Mike, who are best friends. Listen to their conversation.

Ben: What's wrong, Mike? You look angry.

Mike: I am angry! You know Tim, right?

Ben: Yeah. He's in your math class, right?

Mike: Right. Well, after math class this morning, I asked him about the homework. I wanted to get together with him to go over it. He told me that he didn't want to work with me anymore.

Ben: Why? But you guys always do the assignments together. What's wrong?

Mike: Tim said he heard a rumor about me. That I'm homosexual. He said that he couldn't work with a homosexual.

Ben: What? People are saying that you're gay?

Mike: That's what Tim told me. He said there's talk around school. A rumor that we are gay. Not just me, Ben, but you, too. Some people think that both of us are gay.

Ben: I don't understand. You and me? Did you ask him what he thinks?

Mike: Yes, and he told me that people say that we're always together. We're roommates. We eat together. We study together. We go to the movies together, you know?

Ben: But we're best friends. That's what best friends do.

Mike: I know. We've been best friends since high school. That's what I told Tim, and maybe he understands. But he said he couldn't hang out with me because then people would think he's gay, too!

Ben: Mike, you know the truth and I know the truth. I don't care what other people think. You're my best friend.

Mike: I wonder why people believe rumors. We're two men who are very close to each other. Best friends.

Ben: What would people think if we were women, not men?

Mike: What do you mean?

Ben: Well, it's OK for two women to have a close relationship. You know, no one would think they were gay. But two men?

Mike: Hmm, maybe you're right, Ben. Maybe there is a double standard.

··Check Your Understanding ·····················

Answer the questions about Ben and Mike's situation.

1. Does Tim believe the rumor about Ben and Mike?
2. Why does Tim want to stop studying with Mike?
3. Who is Ben's roommate?
4. What do Ben and Mike do together?
5. Why do people think Ben and Mike are gay?

What Do You Think? 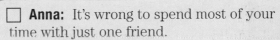 Track 26

A Listen carefully to the opinions of these four people. Who makes the strongest point (even if you disagree)?

☐ **Mark:** You shouldn't believe everything you hear about your friends.

☐ **Anna:** It's wrong to spend most of your time with just one friend.

☐ **Shingo:** You have to be careful how you act with your friends. Someone might start a rumor.

☐ **Iris:** It's difficult to ignore rumors. Sometimes they end up being true.

B Talk about your ideas with a partner.

opinion NETWORK

Do you think	Shingo	is right?
	Iris	
No,	I don't think so.	
	she's totally wrong.	
Yes,	I think he is.	
	she's absolutely right.	

I think Mark has the right idea. You shouldn't believe what you hear. What do you think?

Yes, but I also agree with Iris. It really is difficult to ignore rumors.

Extending the Topic *Best friends: what's OK?*

A Look at the activities in the box. Is it OK for best friends to do these things in your country? What if they are men? Women? A man and a woman?

Activity	Two men	Two women	A woman and a man
hold hands			
hug			
kiss on the cheek			
kiss on the lips			
sleep in the same room			
walk arm in arm			
use the same toothbrush			
give each other presents			
my idea:			
my idea:			

B Share your answers with two or three classmates.

Culture Corner

BASIC

> A: We usually don't see two men holding hands.

> B: Yeah. That's not very common. What about women?

EXTENSION

> C: Sometimes I see women holding hands.

> D: Me, too. I guess that's OK.

C Report your ideas about best friends to the class. Do the other groups agree?

Rumors

by Lindsay Lohan

Saturday steppin' into the club
And it makes me wanna tell the DJ
Turn It Up
I feel the energy all around
And my body can't stop moving to the sound

But I can tell that you're watching me
And you're probably gonna write what you didn't see
Well I just need a little space to breathe
Can you please respect my privacy

I'm tired of rumors starting
I'm sick of being followed
I'm tired of people lying
Saying what they want about me
Why can't they back up off me
Why can't they let me live
I'm gonna do it my way
Take this for just what it is

Sharing My Ideas *It's not fair!*

STEP 1

Choose

Choose a topic that is either something you consider to be unfair to women or something unfair to men. Write your idea in the blank:

....

Examples: Men always do the "heavy" jobs. Men don't have to wear make-up or worry about their appearance. Women are usually the primary childcare provider of the family. Women don't have to be frontline soldiers.

STEP 2

Prepare

Make an outline for your topic. Give reasons why it is unfair.

Speaking notes:

Introduce your topic: ....

First reason: ....

Second reason: ....

Third reason: ....

Conclusion: (A final statement about your topic.) ....

Questions to help you: Do you see this unfairness at home?   At work?   In the government?
Among friends?   Between boyfriends and girlfriends?   Between spouses?

STEP 3

Rehearse

Practice with a partner.

 Listener task: Do you understand your partner's reasons? Should he/she explain more?

STEP 4

Present

Present your topic to a new partner or to a group.

 Listener task: Do you agree? Is the situation unfair?

Presentation Tip:
Remember to write brief notes. You don't need to write complete sentences.

Getting Ready

Work with a partner.
Answer these questions.

1. What is the population of your country?
2. On average, how many children do people in your country have?
3. Does your government control how many children people may have?

Situation Track 27

This is a news program on a radio station. The announcer is reporting a new law about family planning. Listen to the report.

We now turn to national news on FM 88.9 News Central Radio. The prime minister has just signed the new governmental policy on family planning into law. The family-planning policy was approved after six weeks of debate in the government.

Here are the highlights of the new family-planning policy. First, and perhaps most important, all married couples must have at least one child. Let me repeat that for our listeners. All married couples must have at least one child after two years of marriage.

The new law states that there is a penalty for married couples that don't have a child. Each childless couple must pay a fine of 15,000 euros. The money that is collected from childless couples will be paid to parents who have a second child. So if a married couple has a second child, they will get 15,000 euros.

In addition, the new law signed by the prime minister calls for unmarried couples to have a child. After a man and a woman have lived together for two years, they will be considered to be husband and wife. And they have to have a child. If they do not have a child by the third year, they must pay a fine of 15,000 euros.

The prime minister says that this new law will stop the declining population of our country. The number of babies born last year was the lowest in history. The prime minister says we have to increase the country's birth rate or we will slowly lose our population, until there are only old people.

Some people don't like the new family-planning policy. They say that the government should not control the size of families.

And also in the news today on FM 88.9 News Central Radio...

Glossary   **policy** = official rule or law   **highlights** = main ideas   **penalty** = punishment; fine   **childless** − having no children
declining = decreasing in number

Check Your Understanding

Answer these questions about the news report. Circle a, b, or c.

1. All married couples must have:
   a) at least one child.   b) two children.   c) three children.

2. If a married couple has two children, the couple will:
   a) pay a fine of 15,000 euros.   b) receive 15,000 euros.   c) receive a letter from the prime minister.

3. Unmarried couples must have a child:
   a) after living together for one year.   b) after living together for two years.   c) after living together for three years.

4. The prime minister says that this new law will:
   a) raise money for child care.   b) increase the country's birth rate.   c) help childless couples.

5. Some people don't like the new family-planning policy because:
   a) it will increase the country's birth rate.   b) it will hurt poor people.
   c) the government should not control the size of families.

What Do You Think? Track 28

 A   Listen carefully to the opinions of these four people. Check the opinions you agree with.

☐ **Luis:** The government should control the country's population.

☐ **Yeon-Suk:** Children need to have parents who want them. Not all people are good parents!

☐ **Susan:** We need to let people from other countries come to our country. This will increase our population.

☐ **Ken:** The government should not make couples have children. Overpopulation is a major cause of environmental problems.

 B   Discuss your opinions with a classmate.

opinion NETWORK

Do you agree with	Luis's opinion?
	what Ken says?
No,	I don't.
	not really.
	not at all!
Yes,	I do.
	I guess so.
	completely!

I think Luis is wrong. The government shouldn't control the country's population.

Well, I disagree. The government knows what is best for the country.

Extending the Topic *Who should have control?*

A What should your government control and what should it not control?
Check your answers in the following chart.

Government should control:	Agree	Disagree	Depends
the age for getting married.			
how many children you should have.			
the ages for drinking and smoking.			
the number of cars you own.			
what pets you can keep.			
what you should or should not eat.			
what clothes you should or should not wear.			
My idea:			

B Compare answers with two or three classmates. Do you agree?

BASIC

> A: Do you think the government should control the age for getting married?

> B: Definitely! For example, children shouldn't be able to get married.

EXTENSION

> C: I completely agree. What do you think?

> A: Yeah. People shouldn't get married too young.

 **Culture Corner**

Unusual Laws Around the World

- Children may not purchase cigarettes but can smoke them. (Australia)
- Picking up abandoned baggage is an act of terrorism. (England)
- You must pay a fine of $600 if you spit on the sidewalk. (Singapore)
- Prostitution is legal and prostitutes pay taxes like any other businesspeople. (Holland)
- Traffic police are required to report bribes they receive from motorists. (Korea)
- It is illegal to repaint a house without a painting license and the government's permission. (Sweden)
- It is illegal to be drunk on licensed premises (in a pub or bar). (UK)
- You may receive 25 years in prison for cutting down a cactus. (USA, Arizona)

Source: sciforums.com

C Report your group's ideas to the class. According to your group, which things should the government control? Not control?

Sharing My Ideas *A new law for my country*

STEP 1

Choose

You are going to make a new law that is outrageous or funny. Select:

☐ One of the ideas from **Expanding the Topic**. (what pets you can keep, what you should or should not eat, etc.) . . . .

☐ My idea . . . .

STEP 2

Prepare

What is your new law going to be?
Give reasons and examples.

Speaking notes:

My new law: . . . .

Reasons for my new law:

. . . .

. . . .

Examples of how my new law will work:

. . . .

. . . .

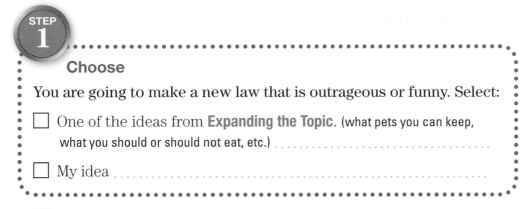

Language Hints:

My new law is...

In our country today,...

I think that we need...

I believe that the new law will...

STEP 3

Rehearse

Practice your presentation.
Work with a classmate.

 Listener task: Is the law funny or outrageous enough? How can it be funnier or more outrageous?

STEP 4

Present

Present your new law to a new partner or to a group.

 Listener task: Do you like the new law? Do you agree? Do you want to argue back? Tell the presenter.

Presentation Tip:
Remember to go back and improve your notes after you practice one time.

Getting Ready

Work with a partner. Answer these questions.

1. In your country, when do children move out of their parents' home?

2. In your country, at what age do most couples get married?

3. How common is it for couples to live together before marriage?

Situation Track 29

Kenji is having a problem with his girlfriend, Mika. He wrote to a website where couples can receive free professional advice on their relationships. Listen to his letter and the response.

My name is Kenji. I am 28 years old and have a good job and a wonderful girlfriend, Mika. I have a problem, and I don't know what to do. I hope you can help me.

Mika and I have been dating for over three years. We love each other very much. I want to marry her, but first I need to save money for two or three years. I want Mika to live with me in my apartment. I think it's a good idea to start living together, anyway and think about marriage later.

She lives at home with her parents. I want Mika to stop living in her parents' house and move into my apartment.

Mika told me that she wants to be with me, but she is worried about her parents. She thinks they are old-fashioned in their beliefs. Her dad told her that a man and a woman should not live together before marriage. She thinks her parents will be very angry with her if she lives with me before we get married.

She is 24 years old and has a good job. She's a grown woman, not a young girl. She should explain to her parents about our situation and then move out of her parents' house and live with me. Mika does not need her parents' permission to live with me. What do you think? Am I right?

Sincerely, Kenji

....

Dear Kenji,

In today's world, women and men live together without being married. Some say that living together before marriage is good because the two people can get to know each other very well. Then, after six months or a year, they might want to get married. Or maybe they will break up!

Others, like Mika's parents, don't agree. They believe it is wrong for a man and a woman to live together without being married.

Here's my advice. As you say, Mika is a grown woman. She can make her own decisions. If you really love her, you should respect her wishes. She doesn't want to hurt her parents. Good luck!

Glossary   **old-fashioned** = out of date; not modern   **permission** = agreement; OK   **break up** = to end a romantic relationship
respect her wishes = to not go against what she wants

•• Check Your Understanding ••••••••••••••••••••

Answer the questions about Kenji's situation.

1. What does Kenji think Mika should do?
2. Does Mika want to live with Kenji before getting married?
3. Why does Kenji want to wait two or three years before getting married?
4. Why is Mika worried about living with Kenji?
5. What advice does Kenji receive?

What Do You Think? Track 30

 A Listen carefully to the opinions of these four people.
Check the opinions that you agree with.

☐ **Anna:** A woman and a man should live together before marriage. That way they can find out if they love each other.

☐ **Iris:** Living together before marriage is wrong. What happens if they have a baby?

☐ **Mark:** When they love each other, it's OK. Love is always right!

☐ **Shingo:** Marriage is old-fashioned. In a few years, no one will get married. So we don't need to be married to live together.

 B Work with a partner.
Talk about the opinions.

What do you think of Anna's opinion?

I agree with her. It's better than getting married and then learning you can't live with that person!

opinion**NETWORK**

What do you think of	Anna's	idea?
	Iris's	opinion?
I think	he makes a good point.	
	she has the right idea.	
I	think so, too.	
	totally agree with you.	

Extending the Topic *Parental influences*

 A Mika thinks it is important to listen to her parents. What would you ask your parents for advice about? Check the decisions you would ask your parents about. Give a reason.

Important life decisions	Agree	Disagree	Reason
choosing a university			....
choosing an area of study			....
choosing a boyfriend or girlfriend			....
deciding to live with my boyfriend/girlfriend before marriage			....
choosing a husband or wife			....
choosing an apartment/house to rent			....
choosing roommates			....
choosing an apartment/house to buy			....
choosing a car to buy			....
deciding which town/city I want to live in			....
my idea:			....

 B Share your reasons with two or three classmates.

BASIC

> A: When would you ask your parents for advice?

> B: I think I would ask them if I was buying a house or apartment.

EXTENSION

> C: Really? Why? I think it should be your own decision. You have to live there.

> B: Your parents probably have experience from buying their own house. They may have some really good advice.

 C Report your group's ideas to the class. Do the other groups agree with you?

 **Culture Corner**

Advice Columns

What are the most common issues?

- Attracting: how to find the right partner
- Commitment: how much to give and when
- Dating strategies: guidelines for the first date
- Dependency: how to break "love addiction"
- Fighting: avoiding arguments with partners and family
- Giving too much: how to deal with one-sided love
- Infidelity: what to do if your partner isn't faithful to you
- Letting go: how to break off a relationship
- Meeting people: how to overcome shyness

Source: salon.com

Sharing My Ideas *Moving in with Kenji*

Mika has decided to ask her parents about moving in with Kenji. They think it's a bad idea, but Mika really wants to live with Kenji before getting married.

STEP 1

Choose

You can be either ☐ Mika or one of Mika's parents, either her ☐ father or ☐ mother. Think of what you will say. How will you convince the other person that you are right?

STEP 2

Prepare

Make notes that support your position. Give examples. Then think about reasons against your position.

My position:	
Reasons SUPPORTING my position	**Examples**
1. (most important)	
2.	
3.	
Reasons AGAINST my position	**My response**
1.	
2.	
3.	

Language Hints:

Compare and contrast reasons for and against:

On the one hand,...

On the other hand,...

You think..., but I think...

STEP 3

Rehearse

Find someone who is the same person as you (Mika, her father, or her mother). Tell your partner the reasons for your position.

 Listener task: What other reasons can you add?

STEP 4

Present

Find someone who is a different person. Present your argument. Try to convince that person you are right.

 Listener task: Take notes when your partner is presenting. Be ready to respond to his/her position.

Presentation Tip:
Remember to pause between sentences. Don't talk too fast or too slowly.

Getting Ready

Work with a partner.
Answer this question.

What's the secret to feeling confident?

☐ A positive attitude

☐ Trying to improve yourself

Situation Track 31

Alicia has fought to control her weight for a long time. Now she has decided to change her attitude because of a group she found on the Internet.

Naomi: Hey, you look great. Are those new clothes?

Alicia: Yeah. I went shopping all day yesterday.

Naomi: Very sexy!

Alicia: Thanks. I've decided to make some big changes in my life. And I mean BIG changes.

Naomi: Wow, what happened?

Alicia: You know, I've always been ashamed of my weight. Always a new diet and always afraid to talk to guys.

Naomi: Yeah, it's been hard for you.

Alicia: Well, I've stopped being afraid. I've decided to be proud of my body. I found a great organization on the Internet. They fight against size discrimination and stereotypes.

Naomi: What do you mean?

Alicia: Well, society teaches us that fat people are ugly, or unhealthy, or that they can't control themselves. It's discrimination!

Naomi: Yeah, I guess that's true.

Alicia: So I went to a meeting last week and the people were great. When I was with them, I felt NORMAL.

Naomi: Well that's cool, but still, it's more healthy not to be overweight.

Alicia: According to this group, it's going on and off diets that causes health problems. That's why I've decided to just focus on eating healthy food.

Naomi: But you've worked really hard NOT to gain more weight. Aren't you worried you'll get bigger?

Alicia: Look, people have to accept that I'm fat and that's OK.

Naomi: You say you're fat? But you hate that word!

Alicia: "Fat" is just an adjective—like "thin" or "tall." I've learned I have nothing to be ashamed of. I have lots of good qualities that are more important than size.

Naomi: Well, it's great that you feel good about yourself. Still, it's a bit hard for me to understand.

Alicia: Oh, Naomi, you've never judged me because of my weight. Don't start now. Don't tell me you're prejudiced, too!

Naomi: I'm sorry. I just want you to be happy.

Alicia: I am. Finally, I am.

Glossary **organization** = group of people with a shared goal   **size discrimination** = treating someone badly or unfairly because they are big   **focus on** = to concentrate on a particular goal   **be prejudiced** = to have an unfair, negative attitude about

Check Your Understanding

Answer the questions about Alicia's situation. Circle a, b, or c.

1. How has Alicia changed?
   a) She lost weight.   b) Her attitude about her body changed.   c) She started a new diet.

2. What made her change?
   a) Shopping for new clothes.   b) Experiencing discrimination.   c) Joining an organization.

3. How does Alicia feel about the word "fat" now?
   a) She hates it.   b) She's not sure how she feels.   c) She accepts it.

4. How does her friend Naomi feel about Alicia's changes?
   a) She's against them.   b) She's in favor of them.   c) She doesn't fully understand them.

5. How does Alicia feel now?
   a) She feels happy.   b) She feels angry.   c) She feels unhappy.

What Do You Think? Track 32

 A
Listen carefully to the opinions of these four people. Who do you agree with most?
Rate the opinions from 1 to 4 (1 = strongly agree, 4 = strongly disagree).

☐ **Susan:** Being healthy is the most important thing— not the shape of your body.

☐ **Yeon-Suk:** People are too worried about appearance. Beauty is inside.

☐ **Luis:** Looking good is important. When you look good, you feel good, too.

☐ **Ken:** Honestly, I think being overweight is just not healthy.

 B Share your opinions with a classmate.

opinion NETWORK

I	agree	with	Yeon-Suk.
	don't agree		Luis.
So do	I.		
Neither do			
I	do, too.		
	don't either.		

I agree with Ken.

So do I. He's absolutely right!

Extending the Topic *Happiness survey*

A Work with a partner. Take this happiness survey. Write your initials in the "opinion box" for each item.

Ideas about happiness	Strongly Agree	Agree	Unsure	Disagree	Strongly Disagree
Everyone should be happy.					
Happiness is an important goal in life.					
I will never be completely happy.					
Human beings are not worthy of being happy.					
I am not sure what makes me happy.					
True happiness comes from within.					
Happiness is a choice that we make.					
Life is very hard and being happy is very difficult.					
Happiness is connected to activities.					
My relationships make me happy.					
My job or school makes me happy.					
My family makes me happy.					

What are the top three factors that make someone happy? Write your initials in three boxes.

- [ ] Giving to others
- [ ] A good attitude
- [ ] The environment around me
- [ ] Religion
- [ ] Good past experiences
- [ ] Having lots of money
- [ ] Good family environment
- [ ] Living in a peaceful country
- [ ] A good job
- [ ] Friends
- [ ] An intimate relationship
- [ ] Inner peace
- [ ] Self-esteem
- [ ] Being able to forgive people
- [ ] A good education

B Now join another pair. Compare your answers. Then ask each other: what are your secrets to happiness?

 **Culture Corner**

C Report your group's ideas to the class. what are your group's secrets to happiness?

Types of Discrimination

- race
- age
- gender
- physical disability
- mental disability
- sexual preference
- religion
- military status
- pregnancy
- height
- weight

Source: EEOC (U.S. Equal Employment Opportunity Commission)

Sharing My Ideas *Self-improvement*

STEP 1

Choose

Select your topic:

- ☐ How to feel confident
- ☐ How to stay healthy
- ☐ How to feel attractive
- ☐ How to make friends

STEP 2

Prepare

Fill in your ideas on the "goal chart."

Speaking notes:

The goal is: .... (use your topic from above)	
Things to do:	Things to avoid: ....
My experiences, my advice, and my conclusion:	

Language Hints:

One thing I did is...

In my experience,...

My advice to everyone is...

If you (do this), you will...

Here are some things that can help you to...

In the end, the most important thing is...

STEP 3

Rehearse

Practice with a classmate.

 Listener task: Give your partner more ideas to put in his/her chart.

STEP 4

Present

Present your topic to a new partner or to a group.

 Listener task: Which idea do you like best? Do you think it will work?

Presentation Tip:
Write brief notes to give your presentation. Don't write out complete sentences.

Getting Ready

Work with a partner.
Answer these questions.

1. Refugees are people who have to leave their countries because of natural disasters, war, or other violence. Are there many refugees in your country?

2. If so, where are they from?

Situation ◖ Track 33

Shen is a university student. He has just heard an announcement from his country's prime minister. The government is planning to give a large amount of money to help African refugees. What does Shen think about this? Listen to his blog and find out.

Hey bloggers, have you heard the latest from Prime Minister Lee? She said that the government will give a huge amount of money to help the refugees in Africa. I think that Ms. Lee has made a lot of mistakes as our prime minister. However, this is one of the dumbest things she has done.

Ms. Lee wants to give our money, money that belongs to us, the people of our country, to help people in Africa. Africa! Africa is thousands of miles away. How many Africans do you know? She said that it is the duty and responsibility of people everywhere to help these starving and homeless people.

I don't agree. I mean, OK, there are starving and homeless refugees in Africa. That's terrible. But did our country make these people refugees? Did we attack them? No, our country is not responsible for making these people refugees.

I think that the United Nations should help. And I think other countries in Africa should help. But the prime minister plans to give our money. Did she ask me? Did she ask you? Our country doesn't have extra money for these things.

There are many starving and homeless people right here in our country. Our government must help them before helping people who live in other countries. Shouldn't our government help our own people first? And then, when there are no more homeless and starving people here, maybe we will think about helping refugees in other places of the world.

Bloggers of our country, let's unite to stop the prime minister from giving away our money. Let's get together and write emails and have marches. Let's help our own people. Please join me. Together we can make a difference!

Glossary   **blog** = personal website where people write their opinions   **bloggers** = people who have their own blogs   **dumb** = stupid
duty = job, task   **starving** = very, very hungry with no food or little to eat   **unite** = to come together; join to work together   **marches** = protests

•Check Your Understanding•

Complete the sentences. Circle a, b, or c.

1. Prime Minister Lee will give .... to help the refugees in Africa.
   a) a huge amount of food   b) a huge amount of money   c) a huge amount of supplies

2. Prime Minister Lee feels that .... are responsible for helping refugees.
   a) all countries   b) only countries with a lot of money   c) only countries that don't have any homeless people

3. Shen believes that his country: ....
   a) is responsible for helping refugees   b) should spend money on its own people first
   c) should support Prime Minister Lee

4. Shen thinks that it's the responsibility of .... to help the African refugees.
   a) the United Nations   b) all wealthy countries   c) only African countries

5. Shen wants to unite with other bloggers to help: ....
   a) his own people   b) refugees all over the world   c) people in Africa

What Do You Think?   Track 34

A

Listen carefully to the opinions of these four people.
Check all of the opinions you agree with.

☐ **Shingo:** Rich countries must help refugees all over the world. They have money to do that.

☐ **Mark:** The United Nations should help refugees. The UN represents all the countries of the world.

☐ **Iris:** A government should help its own people before helping people in other countries. That's the first job of a government.

☐ **Anna:** To tell the truth, I don't know what to do. I don't pay much attention to world affairs.

B   Work with a partner.
Discuss the ideas above.

opinionNETWORK

Iris	has	an interesting idea.
Mark		a strong point of view.
What		do you think?
		is your opinion?
I		basically agree.
		have to think about it.
		don't really agree with that.

> Iris has an interesting idea. What do you think?

> I don't know. I have to think about it.

Extending the Topic *World problems*

 A There are many global problems. Here is a list of some of them. Add to the list. Then think of some ways to solve the problems.

Global Problem	How to solve the problem
refugees	
climate change	
nuclear weapons	
air pollution	
war	
poverty (state of being poor)	
my idea:	
my idea:	

B  Compare ideas with two or three classmates. Do you have the same solutions?

BASIC

> A: What can we do about refugees?

> B: Wealthy countries need to help them. What do you think?

EXTENSION

> C: It's a global problem. I think all countries everywhere should help.

> A: That's a good idea. But I don't think poor countries will want to help.

Culture Corner

World Problems

- Pollution—of the air, the water, the soil
- Natural resources running out or being degraded
- Population growth outstripping resources worldwide
- Unequal distribution of financial resources
- The overwhelming power of multinational corporations over governments
- Nuclear weapons; the imminent danger of worldwide catastrophe
- Military means and thinking as a way of resolving political problems
- Genocides of ethnic groups
- Racism, sexism, homophobia, anti-Semitism
- Rising expectations in third world countries to become modernized

Source: *Hermaneutics* by philospher Richard E. Palmer (mac.edu)

C Report your group's solutions to the class. Which group has the best solutions?

Sharing My Ideas *Let's help!*

STEP 1

Choose

You are the prime minister of your country. You want to persuade your people to help others. Choose one case:

- ☐ Let's help tsunami victims in Asia.
- ☐ Let's help starving people in Africa.
- ☐ Let's help people inside our country first.
- ☐ Let's help (my idea) . . . .

Language Hints:

We must help... because...

I believe that...

It is our responsibility to...

As humans, we need to...

STEP 2

Prepare

For your topic, make an outline of the important points. Give reasons and examples.

Speaking notes:

Introduction: (Explain what you are going to talk about.)

. . . .

Body: (What are your reasons? Give examples.)

. . . .

Conclusion: (Give a summary of your main points.)

. . . .

STEP 3

Rehearse

Find a classmate with the same topic. Then give your presentation to your partner.

 Listener task: What was your partner's main point? Is it a strong one? Will it persuade others who don't agree?

STEP 4

Present

Present to a person with a different topic.

 Listener task: What was the main point? Do you agree?

Presentation Tip:
Show enthusiasm. Use your voice and gestures to help persuade your audience.

Situation Track 35

Akane is Japanese. Her friend Pat is American. They are both 31 years old and have a university education. Both Akane and Pat have some exciting news. Listen to their emails.

Dear Pat,

I have some wonderful news. I'm going to get married in nine months. I'm so excited!

His name is Yoshio. He went to a good university. He has a great job. And his family is very nice. His parents and my parents like each other. All of them think that our marriage will be a good one.

You know, my parents really wanted me to get married. So my mother's friend introduced us. In Japan, this is called *miai*—an arranged meeting of a man and a woman who might be a good match. I like this because in Japan it's hard to meet people for marriage.

Since you're an American, you must think that I love Yoshio very much. Well, I do like him very much and I respect my parents' advice. But I'm not in love with him.

I hope you can come to our wedding.

Akane

Dear Akane,

How exciting! Congratulations. Of course I will come to your wedding. And you must come to mine. That's right. I'm getting married in two weeks!

I know this is a big surprise. It was a surprise for me, too! I met Ted three months ago at a party and, well, it was love at first sight! I introduced myself, we started talking, and we've been together ever since. It's really exciting!

I haven't met his parents, and he hasn't met mine, either. Because we both work and have busy lives, we're going to have a small wedding. I hope our parents can come, but I don't know if they will. My parents want us to wait until we know each other better, but I know in my heart that he's the right one!

Can you come? The wedding will be in San Francisco. Please call me.

Pat

Glossary **good match** = right choice   **love at first sight** = act of falling in love with someone the first time you see him/her
he's the right one = he's the perfect man for me

····Check Your Understanding·····················

Answer the questions about Akane and Pat.

1. How did Akane meet Yoshi?

2. How did Pat meet Ted?

3. When did Pat realize that Ted was "the right one" for her?

4. Will Akane's and Yoshi's parents go to their wedding?

5. Will Pat's and Ted's parents go to their wedding?

What Do You Think? Track 36

Listen carefully to the opinions of these four people. Who has the strongest point? Rank their ideas from 1 to 4 (1 = strongest, 4 = weakest).

☐ **Luis:** Love marriages are better than introduced marriages.

☐ **Susan:** Love marriages end in divorce because people change.

☐ **Ken:** Introduced marriages are comfortable but boring.

☐ **Yeon-Suk:** Introduced marriages are more realistic. Love is a daydream.

 Work with a partner. What do you think of the opinions above?

opinion NETWORK

Whose	idea is	the best?
		the worst?
		the most interesting?
Definitely Susan's. She	really knows	what she's talking about.
	doesn't know	
Probably Ken's. He	has	the right idea.
	doesn't have	a clue.

Whose idea is the best?

Definitely Susan's. Look at the divorce rates around the world.

Extending the Topic *Looking for love*

A Where do men and women find spouses or partners? Look at this list and add your own ideas. Would you look here? Give your reasons.

Location	Would you look here?	Why or why not?
Internet		
university		
nightclub or bar		
work		
fitness center		
parties		
my idea:		

B Compare rankings with a partner. Do you agree?

Extra Activity *Debate*

Work in a group of four. Two of you (A and B) think the Internet is the best place to meet a boyfriend or girlfriend. Two of you (C and D) disagree. Prepare your arguments in pairs (A and B, C and D). Give reasons and examples.

A and B: Give your opinion.
C and D: Explain why you disagree.

> A: We think the Internet is the best place to find a boyfriend or girlfriend.

> B: Our main reason is that you can meet so many people and get to know them a little online. If you like the person, you can meet them in person.

> C: That's true, but the Internet can also be dangerous!

> D: Many people online don't say who they really are. You have to be very careful.

Culture Corner

Marriage and Culture

Indian journalist Anita Jain often writes about cultural issues. Here is an extract from her article about arranged marriages.

The pressure on me to find a husband started very early. A few days after my 1st birthday, within months of my family's arrival in the U.S., I fell out the window of a three-story building in Baltimore. My father recalls my mother's greatest concern after learning that I hadn't been gravely injured: "What boy will marry her when he finds out?" she cried, begging my father to never mention my broken arm—from which I've enjoyed a full recovery—to prospective suitors out of fear my dowry would be prohibitively higher.

Source: nymag.com

Sharing My Ideas *My ideal*

STEP 1

Choose

Select one of the topics below:

☐ My ideal husband/wife ☐ My ideal marriage ☐ My ideal wedding ceremony

STEP 2

Prepare

Think about the characteristics of your ideal. For example, you might want your ideal husband to be well educated. Think about why you want your ideal husband to be well educated. Fill in the blanks in the speaking notes.

Speaking notes:

Introduction: (Say which topic you are going to talk about.)	
Characteristics of your ideal	**Reasons**
Conclusion: (Make a final statement about your ideal.)	

Language Hints:

I want to tell you about my ideal...

To begin with,...

Next,...

Also,...

In conclusion,...

STEP 3

Rehearse

Practice with a classmate.

 Listener task: What are the three characteristics of your partner's ideal?

STEP 4

Present

Present your ideal to a new partner or to a group.

 Listener task: Did your classmates' presentations have... an introduction? a body? a conclusion?

Presentation Tip:
Remember to organize your notes. They should be simple and easy to read.

81

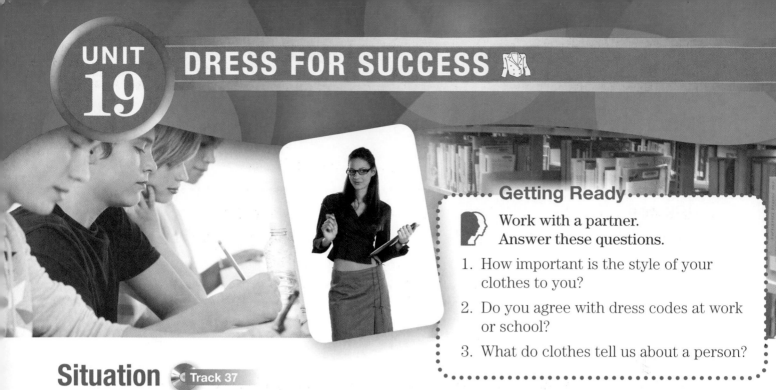

Getting Ready

Work with a partner.
Answer these questions.

1. How important is the style of your clothes to you?
2. Do you agree with dress codes at work or school?
3. What do clothes tell us about a person?

Situation ◖ Track 37

A parent has come to talk to Mr. Nelson, the principal of her daughter's high school. She's upset about Ms. Leeds, one of the teachers. Listen to their conversation.

Mrs. Dudley: Thank you for seeing me. My daughter Mia has me worried about one of her teachers, Ms. Leeds.

Mr. Nelson: Is Mia having trouble in her class?

Mrs. Dudley: No, she loves her class—maybe too much.

Mr. Nelson: I don't understand.

Mrs. Dudley: Well, it's Ms. Leeds's... lifestyle.

Mr. Nelson: Oh, you mean her clothes?

Mrs. Dudley: Yes, her short skirts, dressing like a rock star. Of course, the boys talk about her. But it's also her attitude, trying to act like some kind of rebel.

Mr. Nelson: And her attitude has upset your daughter?

Mrs. Dudley: No, she wants to BE like her! Ms. Leeds told my daughter's class that it's important to be FREE. That's not the kind of example students need.

Mr. Nelson: I admit some people have complained, even some teachers.

Mrs. Dudley: Did you speak to her?

Mr. Nelson: She told me her clothes are none of my business.

Mrs. Dudley: You see? How unprofessional!

Mr. Nelson: She also reminded me that she has excellent student evaluations.

Mrs. Dudley: This is not a popularity contest! A teacher's job is to guide the students.

Mr. Nelson: Well, I think she believes she IS guiding them. She feels students should express themselves.

Mrs. Dudley: A school is a place of learning!

Mr. Nelson: But she is a good teacher.

Mrs. Dudley: Good? So, you're taking her side. Perhaps you like those short skirts, too!

Mr. Nelson: Now, now. I want what's best for the students.

Mrs. Dudley: Really? Well, take strong action or I'm ready to complain to the school board. Others will support me.

Mr. Nelson: I don't think that's necessary. Ms. Leeds can be stubborn. This could create a lot of conflict.

Mrs. Dudley: Mr. Nelson, it's your responsibility! It's time for you to do your job!

Glossary: **rebel** = someone who doesn't follow the rules   **student evaluations** – student feedback about their classes and teachers
Now, now = said in order to calm down someone who is upset   **stubborn** = said about someone who doesn't change his or her mind easily

Check Your Understanding

Are the sentences true or false? Circle T or F.

1. Mrs. Dudley's daughter complained to her mother about Ms. Leeds. T / F
2. Mrs. Dudley doesn't like Ms. Leeds clothes. T / F
3. Mr. Nelson admits that people have complained about Ms. Leeds before. T / F
4. Mrs. Dudley isn't satisfied with how Mr. Nelson has been managing the situation. T / F
5. Mrs. Dudley says she will take action if Mr. Nelson doesn't do something. T / F

What Do You Think? Track 38

A Listen to the opinions of these four people. Check the opinions you agree with.

☐ **Iris:** Ms. Leeds is probably going too far. Mr. Nelson should talk to her again.

☐ **Mark:** It's good for teachers to be stylish. Ms. Leeds should dress however she wants.

☐ **Anna:** I think Ms. Leeds is setting a good example for students. Be free!

☐ **Shingo:** Ms. Leeds is a teacher. She needs to respect the parents' wishes, too.

B Share your opinions with a classmate.

What do you think about the idea that Ms. Leeds is going too far?

I think Iris is right. Ms. Leeds isn't thinking about her effect on the students.

opinion**NETWORK**

What do you think about	the idea that	Ms. Leeds is going to far?
	Iris's opinion that	
I	think she's	right.
		wrong.
	agree	with her.
	disagree	

Extending the Topic *How should teachers act?*

  A Compare Mrs. Dudley's opinion about teachers with yours.

Mrs. Dudley thinks teachers:	My Opinion		
	I agree.	I don't agree.	It depends.
shouldn't wear short skirts.	☐	☐	☐
shouldn't hang out with students.	☐	☐	☐
shouldn't act like rebels.	☐	☐	☐
should listen more to parents.	☐	☐	☐
shouldn't try to be popular.	☐	☐	☐
should be serious.	☐	☐	☐
should act like role models.	☐	☐	☐

  B Share your opinions with two or three classmates. Do you have the same opinions?

BASIC

> A: Mrs. Dudley thinks teachers shouldn't wear short skirts. What do you think?

> B: Well, I agree with her. I think it's distracting when teachers wear short skirts.

EXTENSION

> C: It doesn't matter what the teacher wears. What's important is doing a good job.

> A: I don't know. I think good teachers should dress professionally. It's part of the job.

Culture Corner

Dress Code for Teachers

The following is inappropriate for school employees:

- Dresses and shirts that have cutouts or see-through elements
- Clothing that reveals undergarments
- Clothing that promotes alcoholic beverages, tobacco, the use of controlled substances; depicts violence; is of a sexual nature; or is of a disruptive nature
- Clothing that is tight fitting
- Jewelry affixed to the nose, tongue, cheek, lip, or eyebrow
- Pants not worn on the waist
- Clothing that is provocative, revealing, vulgar, obscene, or profane
- Clothing more than three inches above the top of the knee
- Shirts and blouses that do not cover the back, waist, or midriff
- Shirts and dresses with excessive armpit cutouts

 C Report your group's ideas to the class. What does your group think about how teachers should behave?

Source: Pearson County Schools, North Carolina, USA

Sharing My Ideas *Life lessons*

 STEP 1

Choose

We learn life lessons from different people. Who have you learned from?
Choose who you will talk about.

A person I learned a lot from is .... (my grandfather, a teacher, a friend...)

 STEP 2

Language Hints:

I'd like to tell you about...

I've learned a lot from him/her because...

Let me tell you what happened...

Another thing (I learned) is...

(This experience) made me feel...

Prepare

Make an outline of your story. Use the questions to help you.
Speaking notes:

Introduction: (Say who you are going to talk about.)
....
....

Body: (Describe this person. Explain what you learned from this person. Give examples.)
....
....

Conclusion: (Make a final comment about what this person means to you.)
....
....

Questions to help you: What is this person like?   What did you learn?
How did you learn this?   How do you feel about this person?

 STEP 3

Rehearse

Practice with a classmate.

 Listener task: Do you want to know more about the person? Tell your partner what you'd like to know.

 STEP 4

Present

Present to a new partner or to a group.

Listener task: Write one question you would like to ask.

....
....

Presentation Tip:
Give your presentation without looking at your outline too much.

Getting Ready

Work with a partner.
Answer these questions.

1. Does your country have the death penalty—killing someone who commits a terrible crime?

2. Do you think the death penalty is right?

3. If a country has the death penalty, how should it be done?
   a) using an electric chair   b) by drugs   c) by hanging

Situation Track 39

Have you ever wished that someone were dead? This mother did. Listen to her story.

My heart jumped with joy when he was dead. I knew then, when the electricity was sent into that man's body, that I would finally have peace.

Am I a monster? Am I thirsty for blood? Do I get excited when people are killed? No, no, no! I am not a monster. I am a mother whose 18-year-old son was killed during a robbery.

Before Wang was killed, I had not thought much about capital punishment. Maybe I thought it was wrong. After all, killing someone who has killed someone else really doesn't help much. The other person is still dead, and killing the murderer just adds to the violence.

But that all changed when my only son was killed. It happened five years ago. Wang was working at a grocery store. He had just finished high school and was going to go to a good university in a month. He was working to earn money to help pay for his education.

Two men entered the store. They told my son to take all the money from the cash registers and put it in a bag. He did this. Then they ordered Wang to open the safe. Wang told them that he did not have the key. One of the men had a gun and threatened to shoot Wang. My son pleaded with him and told him that only the owner had the key. The gunman then shot him five times in the face and heart. My son died instantly.

Both robbers were captured. The one who shot my son was sentenced to death in the electric chair. I asked to see him die. I wanted to be there. I needed to be there. My son's death had to be repaid.

So I watched when they strapped him in. I saw him begging for his life. Good, I thought, beg all you can. You must die for what you did.

I think about capital punishment often now. Killing is wrong. But if you kill, you should pay with your own life. It is the only way we can stop all the violence.

Glossary   **death penalty** = the legal punishment of death   **monster** = very, very bad person   **threaten** = to promise to do something bad to someone   **plead** = to beg   **capture** = to take prisoner   **capital punishment** = killing someone who has committed a crime

··Check Your Understanding·····

Answer the questions about Wang and his mother.

1. Who was killed during a robbery?

2. Why did the robber shoot Wang?

3. Did Wang have the key?

4. What happened to the robber who shot Wang?

5. Why did Wang's mother want to see the robber die?

What Do You Think? Track 40

 A Listen carefully to the opinions of these four people. Which person makes the strongest point? Rate their opinions from 1 to 4 (1 = strongest point, 4 = weakest point).

☐ **Susan:** I understand Wang's mother. This is the only way she can have peace.

☐ **Luis:** I understand Wang's mother, but life in prison is better. Maybe the murderer will change.

☐ **Yeon-Suk:** I don't understand Wang's mother. Killing is never right, not even for a son's murderer.

☐ **Ken:** Wang's mother is right. The man killed her son. He deserves to die.

 B Work with a classmate.
Discuss the opinions above.

opinionNETWORK

How	do you feel	about	Susan's opinion?
			Yeon-Suk's point?
I	sympathize	with her.	
	understand	what she means.	
	know	how she feels.	
I	don't understand	her.	
	don't get		

How do you feel about Susan's opinion?

I sympathize with the mother. She lost her son. What do you think?

Extending the Topic *Just punishment*

A What punishment would you give in these situations?

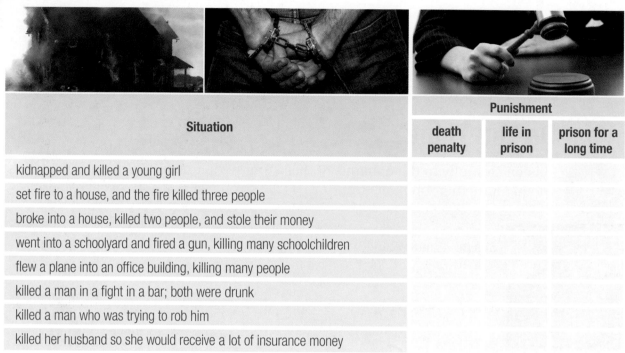

Situation	Punishment		
	death penalty	life in prison	prison for a long time
kidnapped and killed a young girl			
set fire to a house, and the fire killed three people			
broke into a house, killed two people, and stole their money			
went into a schoolyard and fired a gun, killing many schoolchildren			
flew a plane into an office building, killing many people			
killed a man in a fight in a bar; both were drunk			
killed a man who was trying to rob him			
killed her husband so she would receive a lot of insurance money			

B Work with two or three classmates.
Do you have the same answers?

BASIC

> A: When a person kidnaps and kills a young girl, what should happen to him?

> B: I think he should get the death penalty. He deserves to die.

EXTENSION

> C: That's a little strong. I think he should spend the rest of his life in jail. What do you think?

> A: I agree. Life in prison is the best punishment for him.

Culture Corner

The Death Penalty

For centuries the death penalty, often accompanied by barbarous refinements, has been trying to hold crime in check; yet crime persists.
- ALBERT CAMUS, Resistance, Rebellion and Death

Government... can't be trusted to control its own bureaucrats or collect taxes equitably or fill a pothole, much less decide which of its citizens to kill.
- HELEN PREJEAN, Dead Man Walking

If we are to abolish the death penalty, I should like to see the first step taken by my friends the murderers.
- ALPHONSE KARR, Les Guêpes, Jan. 31, 1849

C Report your group's ideas to the class. Which situations deserve the worst punishment?

Source: freenet-homepage.de/dpinfo/quotes.htm

Sharing My Ideas *You be the judge!*

STEP 1

Choose

Look at the situations in **Extending the Topic**. Select one of them and explain your reasons for the punishment you chose.

Language Hints:

I'm going to talk about...

In this situation,...

I believe this person deserves... because...

In conclusion, I feel that this crime...

STEP 2

Prepare

Make an outline for your presentation.

Speaking Notes:

Introduction: (Say which situation you are going to talk about. Give more information about the situation. Use your imagination!)

....

....

Body: (Explain what the punishment should be and why.)

....

....

Conclusion: (Make a final point on the crime and the punishment.)

....

....

STEP 3

Rehearse

Practice saying your ideas silently one time. Try to improve your notes. Then practice with a partner.

 Listener task: Is there anything your partner should add? Is there anything your partner should take out?

STEP 4

Present

Present your ideas to a new classmate or to a group.

 Listener task: Do you agree with the presenter? Is the punishment correct? Why or why not?

Presentation Tip:
Remember to make eye contact with your audience!

Appendix
Personal Opinions

Read each person's opinion about the topic. Fill in the missing words. Note: These are only summaries of the speakers' opinions. To watch the video clips and read the full scripts, go to www.impactseries.com/issues.

Unit 1 – First Impressions
Sara

realize   wrong   yourself   date   pretended

In my opinion, intelligence is sexy in a woman. Changing yourself is definitely _____, I would say. I have female friends who do that all the time, trying not to act intelligent. When you do that, it may be really easy to get a _____. But the problem is they date that person for a while and eventually they _____ it was the wrong man. And finally they break up because they _____ they were a different person. If you want the right man, you have to be _____.

Unit 2 – Traffic Jam
Derek

transportation   rise   lives   living   future

Oil prices are likely to continue rising over the next several years. And while the world population is steadily increasing, several countries are experiencing a rise in their standard of living. So it seems that the number of cars and oil consumption is going to continue to _____. As a result, problems like traffic congestion and air pollution will become problems as well for the _____. Governments will have to intervene to help solve both the air pollution and traffic congestion. My guess is that this kind of intervention will become part of the norm of our daily _____. Dealing with these traffic issues and higher costs of _____, due to higher oil consumption, means that things such as public funded _____ will have to be part of our daily routine.

Unit 3 – Who Needs the Local Language?
Scott

respect   language   place   culture   excuse

If you go anywhere to live for an extended period of time, you need to make the effort to learn that local _____. It shows a lot about your willingness to learn about the _____ and I pretty much can guarantee that if you take the time to learn that language, the people around you, whether or not they speak English, will _____ you more. That has been my experience in living in Japan, so I would urge all people to make an effort to learn the local language. If you've lived in a _____ for only one year or something like that, then there's no way you can help it, but after four years or so, there's no _____ not to try.

Unit 4 – Getting Ahead
Mike

compromise   values   environment   balance   raise

Family disputes are always a big problem. People often don't agree about most things, but when it's in a family unit, it's even more problematic. The problem here is that a brother and sister have different _____. One sees a good home as being very important. The other sees a good education as being very important. I think both are equally important. You need to _____ between the two.

Private school is not necessarily always the best way to go. Sometimes public school is better. It depends on how you _____ your child. Family values still can be instilled whether you send your child to a private school or a public school. What you have to do is create a good home _____. What this particular brother and sister need to do is sit down and really talk about what's important to both of them, and find a _____.

Unit 5 – Forever Single
Mei

forming   share   secure   close   trust

In my opinion, if two people love each other and want to stay together, they should get married. Of course, marriage requires taking on lots of responsibility. Basically, you have to _____ almost everything. And you really have to _____ someone and you really have to respect that person in order to be able to share everything, because you have to share not only the good things but also the bad things, too.

I've been married for seven years and my husband and I don't have children, but I don't feel like I'm just living with someone. I feel like I live with my husband and we are _____ a family. I also feel very close to his parents. In a way, I think they are my parents, too, and I feel my parents are his parents as well. For example, if anyone in our family gets sick, we really worry and take care of each other. And we feel very close and _____ in that way. So I think this is very different from two people just living together. We feel more _____ and secure.

Unit 6 – What Are Friends For?
Sun-Hi

careful   trust   help   difficult   worsen

In this case, there would be a higher chance of me lending him the money if I knew his reason. If I believed his reason, if I believed the money would _____ him solve the situation, I would lend him the money. But if the reason were something like gambling, I think it would _____ his situation, so I would not lend him the money.

And also money can be a tricky issue between friends, so I think he should be _____ in that regard as well. But it seems that these two friends have a friendship built upon _____, so I think they will make it through. Personally,

I have never asked my friends for money because I believe it would put them in a _____ situation as well.

Unit 7 – What's for Dinner?
Vania

health   balance   fast   difficult   love   solve

I have to admit, I love meat, especially beef. And I also love _____ food. I realize that too much meat, or too much fast food, is not good for your _____. Personally, I tried to be a vegetarian once, but frankly I just couldn't do it. I really wanted to eat meat. And everywhere I went, there was meat in front of me, so I found it was really _____ to be a vegetarian. But I think it's important to strike a _____ between eating vegetables and meat.

As for the environmental issues, I really hope they can _____ this issue related to raising animals. But to tell you the truth, just from a personal perspective, I don't think I can stop eating meat because I really _____ it.

Unit 8 – Cyber Bullying
Mike

authority   weak   deal   tell   worry

In schools bullying has always been a problem. It definitely was when I was a student. What students need to remember is that bullies are basically _____ and insecure. They take out their problems on other people. People who are bullied need to gain more confidence in themselves, and not _____ about these things. For example, if you get a strange email, so what? I think you just have to ignore it, move on, deal with it.

But, of course, when it gets to be too much, as sometimes it does, people need to _____ other people about the problem. You can tell your teachers, you can tell your

parents. Talking with your friends, your peers, is a good idea, but friends can't always help you _____ with these things. You need to talk to someone in a position of _____, someone who can effect a real outcome.

Unit 9 – Taking Care of Father
Stacy-Ann

open   respond   parents   answer   allow

This is a tough issue. I would personally want to open my home to my family whenever it's needed. But what I do have to consider is how anybody that lives with me, whether it's my husband or my kids, how they feel about me opening my home to my family. I'd want to know how they would _____ to having another guest in the house. Opening the discussion would probably lead to a more rational _____ or maybe open the family up to _____ this family member into your home.

I wouldn't want my _____ living in a nursing home or anything like that. And they wouldn't want me putting them in a nursing home either, so in this situation, I would have to _____ up my home to my parents.

Unit 10 – Why Go to School?
Justin

lives   partner   brains   wrong   future

In my opinion, these four years of university are supposed to be a training ground for our _____. We have to spend these four years learning, studying, growing, treating our brains like the gardens that they are. If we don't, then we will spend the rest of our _____ with no conversation, no interests, no hobbies.

And in the end, when we want to find a _____ for life or interesting friends, we won't be able to find any. Why not? Because we won't have any powers of conversation ourselves, so we won't be able to discuss anything intelligently. If we go to see a film and somebody says, "What do you think of that film?", we'll say, "Huh, I don't know." So, in my opinion, Mariko is completely _____. She should dedicate herself to her studies. She should grow. And she should think about the _____.

Unit 11 – An International Relationship
Gillian

together   married   decided   jobs   separate

In my view, all young people, and particularly young women, should get experience, life experience. I would recommend to anyone who's just graduating from college, travel a little, have work experience in different places, even take on different _____. I would not recommend people rush into committed relationships, or consider getting _____ that young.

I have a friend who had a very close intimate relationship with her boyfriend at university. When graduation came around, they _____ to go different ways, but they kept in touch. My friend went to the States, from England, for two years, met many different people, had different experiences. At the end of two years, she met up with her boyfriend again, and then they decided they had had their _____ experiences, and they wanted to be _____. Don't rush things!

Unit 12 – Too Little, Too Late
Stacy-Ann

problem   consume   energy   responsible   limit   industry

This is a complex situation. You have to look at it from many different angles. First of all, you have to think about the way we _____ products, our modes of transportation, the way we consume _____, and the way we use our natural resources. If we were able to _____ our uses of these elements, then we might have a better environment.

As for overpopulation, it's not necessarily a _____. It becomes a problem when we have this kind of consumerism, where people consume more than they need. And when we have an _____ that wants to provide for these people. Personally, I think we should limit consumerism and give everybody an awareness of how to be _____ for the environment around them.

Unit 13 – Ben and Mike
Steve

believe   gossip   realize   mean   confused   similar

Unfortunately, this is a very typical situation. People are people. No matter where you are, whatever country you're in, someone will _____ about somebody. I don't know why it happens, but it does.

Related to this particular situation, I had a _____ thing happen to me. I had left my email program open by mistake. I guess I had forgotten to close it and I didn't _____ it at the time. Apparently, what happened was someone sent a friend of mine, a male friend, an email from my computer saying that I wanted to go out with him.

So this friend came up to me a few days later and said, "Steve, forget about it. I'm not like that!" And I said, "What do you _____?" I had no idea what he was talking about. And he didn't tell me and I was really _____! And then a couple of days later, he said that I had sent him an email, asking him for a date. And I said, "No way. That wasn't me!" And he still didn't _____ me.

Unit 14 – Government Control
Todd

encourage   enough   favor   pay   idea   problem

This concept of government control is a very interesting idea. Many countries have a population problem, while other countries don't have _____ people. They have aging societies. In this sense, trying to regulate the population seems like a good _____. I am in favor of the government giving some money when children are born because children do cost so much money. And in developed countries there seems to be a _____ with the aging society—not having enough children.

Now in other countries there are too many children, but I'm not in _____ of the government telling them they must not have children. Advising, yes, but not telling them. So as far as fining childless couples, I think the government is going too far there. Basically, the government has to strike the right balance to _____ those countries that need more children to have children, to encourage the countries that have too many children not to have children. But make them _____ fines? I think that's going overboard a bit.

Unit 15 – Living Together
Derek

changed   understand   step   mistake   opinion

If people want to cohabitate before marriage, it's really up to the individuals who are involved in the relationship to decide. Obviously, society as a whole, and ultimately parents are going to have an _____ about this issue. But still it's up to those two people. If they want to take their relationship to the next _____, but maybe they don't feel they're ready for that large a commitment, then cohabitation might be the way to take the relationship to a higher level.

Parents may not be satisfied with the decision, but they need to _____ that their children are growing up in an era different from their own. The value systems have _____. So for two people to live together before marriage could open the doors for them to explore the relationship better. And ultimately, it might help them avoid making a _____. You know, in a lot of societies the divorce rates are fifty percent.

Unit 16 – Size Discrimination
Andrea

believe   appearance   reason   OK   clothes

These days we're told that beauty is having a certain kind of hairstyle or wearing a certain kind of _____. But I really feel that the real root of beauty lies in self-confidence. Once you have that, your general physical _____ will start to match your psychological appearance. If you really think about it, the most beautiful people you know are those people that kind of exude self-confidence and _____ in themselves.

For this _____, even though the young woman in this scenario may not be changing physically, people will see her in a different light, because she believes a different thing about herself. And that's that she is who she is. She's not dissatisfied with that. She's _____ with that. And I think that's the secret to success.

Unit 17 – Who Will Help Them?
Justin

day   choice   people   sleep   ourselves

Yes, we have to look after ourselves, our family, our friends. And if we're a government, we have to look after our _____. But let's think about this. Imagine you have a choice: you can help someone or you can refuse to help someone. Can you sleep at night, having made the _____ not to help them? I don't think you can. I think governments are just an extension of individuals, and I think governments also need to _____ well at night. So while we may want to keep all the money to help _____, I think it's very important to be kind and generous to help others, just as one _____ we may need help, too.

Unit 18 – Finding the Right One
Mei

introduced   happy   love   forever   together   safe

Which is better—introduced marriages or love marriages? Personally, I think an introduced marriage is a _____ way to meet someone. When I was younger I thought that it was very unromantic, and I wasn't in favor of it. But now I think it's a good idea because I have a friend who was introduced to her husband through her parents and she didn't know him at all. But they got married right away and they have been married for almost ten years. And to me they look very _____. They have two children. She has many hobbies that her husband supports and I think that they _____ each other, too.

But there is no guarantee that you can be in love _____. One thing to remember is that loving each other doesn't necessarily mean that you'll be happy _____. So, in this sense, I think a love marriage is good but _____ marriage can also be good.

Unit 19 – Dress for Success
Sara

expression   uniforms   interested   boring   who

I think this is an interesting situation. As for me, I would love to have had a stylish teacher. When I was in high school, we all had to wear dark-colored _____ and the teachers wore these very simple clothes. And to tell the truth, we found it quite _____.

I think that the way people dress is an _____ of who they are. And I think that the students want to know _____ their teachers are. You know, some of the subjects in high school are not all that interesting, so I think if you know your teachers more personally, it can help the students become more _____ in their subjects.

Unit 20 – A Mother's Story
Scott

wrong   deal   approve   sense   execution

I'm a little skeptical about this. The woman in the story said that it made her feel better when she saw her son's killer die. But actually studies have shown that when people like this actually watch the _____, they may in the short term feel good, but the long-term effects aren't good at all. Nobody is actually psychologically prepared to _____ with this.

Generally speaking, I don't _____ of the death penalty. I don't think that a life for a life makes _____. The state is just as barbaric as the killer if you do that. And then also from the psychological point of view of those who were done _____ by the killing, in the end, it doesn't make anyone feel good. So I don't agree with the mother's stance.

Vocabulary

Study these vocabulary words before or after you work on each unit.

 Definitions come from *Longman Dictionary of Contemporary English*.

Unit 1

appreciate – to understand how good or useful someone or something is

brilliant – extremely clever or skillful

confident – sure that you have the ability to do things well or deal with situations successfully

cool – used to say that you agree with something, that you understand it

flirt – to behave toward someone in a way that shows that you are sexually attracted to them, although you do not really want a relationship with them

graduate research – serious study of a subject, done at a university after completing a first degree

idiot – a stupid person or someone who has done something stupid

ignore – to deliberately pay no attention to something or someone

major – the main subject that a student studies at college or university

physics – the science concerned with the study of physical objects and substances, and of natural forces such as light, heat and movement

pretend – to behave as if something is true when in fact you know it is not, in order to deceive people or for fun

talent – a natural ability to do something well

Unit 2

common – existing in large numbers

commute – to regularly travel a long distance to get to work

fee – an amount of money that you pay to do something

inconvenient – causing problems, often in a way that is annoying

pollution – the process of making air, water or soil dangerously dirty and not suitable for people to use, or the state of being dangerously dirty

public transportation – means of travel that are available for anyone to use (not private)

resident – someone who lives or stays in a particular place

step by step – a step-by-step plan or method explains or does something carefully and in a particular order

traffic jam – a long line of vehicles on a road that cannot move or can only move very slowly

Unit 3

admire – to look at something and think how beautiful or impressive it is

appreciate – used to thank someone in a polite way or to say that you are grateful for something they have done

colleague – someone you work with, used especially by professional people

efficiency – the quality of doing something well and effectively, without wasting time, money or energy

energy – the physical and mental strength that makes you able to do things

exotic – something that is exotic seems unusual and interesting because it is related to a foreign country

foreign staff – people from other countries who work for an organization

in theory – something that is true in theory is supposed to be true, but might not really be true or might not be what will really happen

local staff – the citizens of the country who work for an organization

silly – stupid in a childish or embarrassing way

would you care to do something? – [spoken formal] used to ask someone politely whether they want to do something

Unit 4

conflict – a state of disagreement or argument between people, groups or countries

get ahead – make progress in your job or education

good intentions – a plan or desire to do something good or kind

hold back – to keep from advancing or going ahead or doing something

invest – to use a lot of time and effort or spend money in order to make something succeed

jealousy – feeling angry and unhappy because someone has something that you wish you had

neighborhood – the area around you or around a particular place, or the people who live there

special treatment – when one person is treated better than another

stuck – impossible or unable to move from a particular position

Unit 5

believe in (something) – to think that something is effective or right

bring up – to look after and influence a child until he or she is grown up [=raise]

die out – to disappear or stop existing completely

divorce – the legal ending of a marriage

divorce rate – the number of examples of divorce within a certain period

dreamer – someone who has ideas or plans that are not practical

fool – someone who has done something stupid

peer pressure – a strong feeling that you must do the same things as other people of your age if you want them to like you

ruin – to spoil or destroy something completely

unrealistic – ideas, plans or hopes that are not reasonable or sensible

Unit 6

be there for (someone) – to be available to help

depressed – not at all happy; sad

escape – to get away from a place without permission

get along well – if two or more people get along, they have a friendly relationship

hang out with – to spend a lot of time with particular people

hit it off – if two people hit it off, they like each other as soon as they meet

horrible – very unpleasant and often frightening, worrying or upsetting

lend – to let someone borrow money or something that belongs to you for a short time

Unit 7

destroy – damage something so badly that it no longer exists or cannot be used or repaired

environment – the air, water, and land on Earth, which can be harmed by human activities

export – to sell goods to another country

in part – to some degree, but not completely [= partly]

lecture – a long talk on a particular subject that someone gives to a group of people, especially to students in a university

protein – one of several natural substances that exist in food such as meat, eggs, and beans

rain forest – a tropical forest with tall trees that are very close together, growing in an area where it rains a lot

rich in – containing a lot of something

Unit 8

be mean to (someone) – treat someone very badly or intend to hurt someone

blog – a web page that is made up of information about a particular subject

competition – a situation in which people try to be more successful than other people

embarrassing – making you feel ashamed, nervous or uncomfortable

figure (someone/something) out – to think about a problem or situation until you find the answer or understand what has happened

overreact – to react to something with too much emotion

popular – liked by a lot of people

that's sick – that's strange or cruel

upset – unhappy and worried because something unpleasant or disappointing has happened

victim – someone who has been attacked

Unit 9

commute – to regularly travel a long distance to get to work

lease – a legal agreement that allows you to use an apartment or building for a period of time, in return for rent

nursing home – a place where people who are old and ill can live and be looked after

only child – a person who has no sisters or brothers

retired – having stopped working, usually because of your age

selfish – caring only about yourself and not about other people

tiny – extremely small

vague – unclear because someone does not give enough detailed information or does not say exactly what they mean

(something is) up – if something is up, someone is feeling unhappy because they have problems, or there is something wrong in a situation

Unit 10

complain – to say that you are annoyed, not satisfied or unhappy about something or someone

credit – a successfully completed part of a course at a university or college

graduate – obtain a degree, especially a first degree, from a college or university

have a balance in life – to make sure that you work hard and also have a good social life and family life

have in common – have the same interests or attitudes as someone else

honor – to show publicly that someone is respected and admired

minimum – the minimum number is the smallest that is possible, allowed or needed

miserable – making you feel very unhappy or uncomfortable

priority – the thing that you think are most important and that need attention before anything else

social life – what you do when you are not working or studying; time spent with friends

succeed – to do what you tried or wanted to do

Unit 11
amazing – excellent, fantastic, wonderful, great

genius – someone who has an unusually high level of intelligence, skill or ability

have connections – to know people who can help you

make a living – earn enough money to pay for your life expenses

precious – valuable and important and should not be wasted

starving artist – an artist who believes that making art is more important than earning money

support – to provide enough money for someone to pay for all the things they need

truly – used to emphasize that the way you are describing something is really true

visa – an official mark put on your passport that gives you permission to temporarily enter or leave a foreign country

Unit 12
be blind to something – be blind to something to completely fail to notice or realize something

be deaf to something – to be unwilling to hear or listen to something

climate change – change in weather on a planet over a long period of time

disposable – intended to be used once or for a short time and then thrown away

ice cap – an area of thick ice that permanently covers the North and South Poles

ignore – deliberately pay no attention to something that you have been told or that you know about

limited – not very great in amount or number

natural resources – things that exist in nature and can be used by people, for example oil and trees

ordinary – average, common, or usual, not different or special

pay attention – to notice and be concerned or think about something

toxin – a poisonous substance, especially one that is produced by bacteria and causes a particular disease

wasted – ruined or destroyed

Unit 13
close – if two people are close, they like or love each other very much

double standard – a rule or principle that is unfair because it treats one group of people more severely

gay – if someone, especially a man, is gay, they are sexually attracted to people of the same sex

get together – if people get together, they meet in order to spend time with each other

go over – review or repeat something in order to make sure it is correct

homosexual – if someone, especially a man, is homosexual, they are sexually attracted to people of the same sex [= gay]

rumor – information or a story that is passed from one person to another and which may or may not be true

spread (a rumor) – to become known about or used by more and more people

Unit 14
approve – to officially accept a plan or proposal

childless – having no children

debate – discussion of a particular subject that often continues for a long time and in which people express different opinions

decline – to decrease in quantity or importance

fine – money that you have to pay as a punishment

highlights – the most important, interesting, or enjoyable parts of something

on average – based on a calculation about how many times something usually happens

outrageous – very shocking and extremely unfair or offensive

penalty – a punishment for breaking a law, rule, or legal agreement

policy – a way of doing something that has been officially agreed and chosen by a political party, business or other organization

Unit 15
break up – if a marriage or relationship breaks up, the people in it separate and do not live together any more

common – happening often and to many people or in many places

grown man/woman – an adult man or woman, used especially when you think someone is not behaving as an adult should

in today's world – in the current social conditions

live with – to live in the same house as someone and have a sexual relationship with them without being married

old-fashioned – not considered to be modern or fashionable any more

permission – when someone is officially allowed to do something

professional advice – advice from someone who knows a lot about a subject

respect – to be careful not to do anything against someone's wishes or rights

Unit 16
ashamed of – feeling embarrassed and guilty because of something you have done

attitude – the opinions and feelings that you usually have about something

confident – sure that something will happen in the way that you want or expect

focus on – to give special attention to one particular thing

judge someone – to form or give an opinion about someone after thinking carefully about all the information you know about them

organization – a group such as a club or business that has formed for a particular purpose

prejudiced – having an unreasonable dislike of someone or something

size discrimination – treating someone unfairly because of the size of their body

stereotype – a belief or idea of what a particular type of person or thing is like. Stereotypes are often unfair or untrue

Unit 17
attack – deliberately use violence to hurt a person or damage a place

blog – a web page that is made up of information about a particular subject

blogger – a person who has his/her own blog

dumb – stupid (informal)

duty – something that you have to do because it is morally or legally right [= obligation]

huge – extremely large in size, amount or degree

make a difference – make a/the difference to have an important effect or influence on something or someone

march – an organized event in which many people walk together to express their ideas or protest about something

responsibility – a duty to be in charge of someone or something

starve – to suffer or die because you do not have enough to eat

unite – if different people or organizations unite, or if something unites them, they join together in order to achieve something:

Unit 18
arranged – planned or organized for a particular purpose

congratulations – when you tell someone that you are happy because they have achieved something or because something nice has happened to them

know in my heart – to know intuitively, to feel confident about

love at first sight – the act of falling in love with someone the first time you see them

match – a situation in which something is suitable for something else

spouse – a husband or wife

the right one – the right thing, person or method is the one that is most suitable or effective

Unit 19
complain – to say that you are annoyed, not satisfied, or unhappy about something or someone

dress code – a set of rules, laws, or principles that tell people what clothes they can wear and not wear

evaluation – a judgment about how good, useful, or successful something is [= assessment]

go too far – to do something that is not acceptable because it is excessive

now, now – used to make someone calm or comfort them when they are angry or upset

rebel – someone who opposes or fights against people in authority

responsibility – a duty to be in charge of someone or something

stubborn – determined not to change your mind, even when people think you are being unreasonable

stylish – attractive in a fashionable way

take action – to do a specific thing that needs to be done, especially after discussing it

Unit 20
capital punishment – punishment which involves killing someone who has committed a crime

capture – to catch a person and keep them as a prisoner

cash register – a machine used in shops to keep the money in and record the amount of money received from each sale

death penalty – the legal punishment of death

deserve something – to have earned something by good or bad actions or behavior

jump with joy – to be extremely happy and pleased

kidnap – to take someone somewhere illegally by force, often in order to get money for returning them

monster – someone who is very cruel and evil

plead – to ask for something that you want very much, in a sincere and emotional way [= beg]

sentence – if a judge sentences someone who is guilty of a crime, they give them a punishment

sympathize – to feel sorry for someone because you understand their problems

threaten – to say that you will cause someone harm or trouble if they do not do what you want

Dynamic Conversation Series

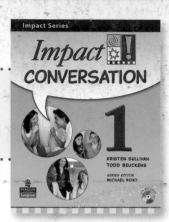

Cutting-Edge Discussion Series

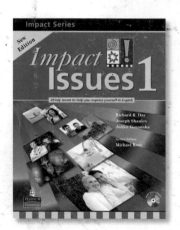

Innovative Listening Series

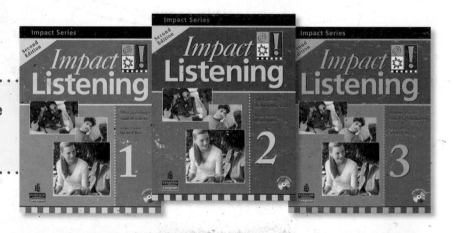

Coursebook Series

Grammar and Vocabulary Skills

www.impactseries.com